WISE WOMAN WITHIN

LIVING FROM THE WISDOM WITHIN

Endorsements

Wise Woman Within is sure to bless and encourage women of all ages!

—**Roma Downey**, actress, producer, and *New York Times* bestselling author.

In *Wise Woman Within*, Jean and Jess have given us an eye-opening roadmap for the interior journey we now find ourselves navigating in this challenging new world where genuine connection is increasingly hard to find. With timeless truths and surprising insights, they carry us safely through a fascinating exploration of faith into the deeper places where joy, healing, and true peace reside. Wise Women indeed!

—**Martha Williamson**, head writer and executive producer of the CBS television series *Touched by an Angel*

In *Wise Woman Within*, Jean Barnes and Jessica Wrasman share stories of how God drew them to Him through their experiences with struggles and pain. In seeking God, they grew to value a daily habit of solitude, prayer, and Bible study, and began hearing the gentle whisper of Jesus and embracing his wisdom. *Wise Woman Within* is not to be missed!

—**Steve Arterburn**, founder of New Life Ministries, best-selling author and host of *New Life Live!*

What an amazing privilege to glean from the words of these two wise women! Reading *Wise Woman Within* is like sitting down for a cup of tea with personal mentors—the kind who kick off their shoes and share their personal struggles along with any triumphs. No masks allowed here, no wrapping things up with a perfect bow on top—you will feel seen and known, not alone. And you will experience hope coming from the knowledge that God delights to call out this wise woman within—he created her for this! Filled with thoughtful and tangible practices with which to do this inner work, *Wise Woman Within* will bless you deeply. Be on the lookout for God's care and kindness toward you throughout this book.

—**Jen Simmons**, licensed professional counselor, church planter, and pastor's wife

In *Wise Woman Within*, two wise women, representing different age groups, share their stories of life's struggles and blessings. Through power of purpose and an unbreakable connection with God, this eloquent and honestly written work transcends generations and brings empowering words to women of all ages.

—**Anne-Frans Van Villet**, author of *Animal Energy Therapy Project*, animal behaviorist and holistic energy therapist

Wise Woman Within reads like a community coming to the table where you sit, swapping stories and wisdom, getting practical, and pausing in prayer. Jess and Jean have forged together their lives and the many ways Jesus has taught, led, and transformed them into a tool to help us "carve out our true selves from the rubble so we may offer diamonds." Yes. Amen. Thank you for writing this book.

—**Darcy Luetzow Staddon**, cross-cultural worker, singer, songwriter, and poet

In *Wise Woman Within*, Jess and Jean make a dynamic team, opening many layers, like a well-baked cake, of spiritual insight, heartfelt honesty, and clear exploration of their emotional landscapes. It was a joy, and at times terrifying, to hear how those landscapes are all fodder for God's handiwork, to mold and shape us. Personal and intimate in every single way, I absolutely wanted to keep reading, to savor each golden morsel, knowing I was being led to grow closer to Christ and have more of my hunger filled by him.

—**Kim Oberheu,** founder, The Swanky Group

Wise Woman Within will inspire you to live a life pursuing authenticity. As you become more intimate with Jesus, He will transform your life, masks will be lifted, and your true identity will emerge. This book is a must read! *WWW* is the very soul of who we are and will inspire you toward more joyful and peaceful relationships, stronger family connections, and ultimately, a life reflecting the light of Jesus.

—**Kathy McGill**, Bible study leader

WISE WOMAN WITHIN

LIVING FROM THE WISDOM WITHIN

Jean S. Van Dyck Barnes, ME
Jessica Wrasman, MA

ELK LAKE PUBLISHING INC

PUBLISHING THE POSITIVE
Plymouth, Massachusetts

COPYRIGHT NOTICE

Wise Woman Within: Living from the Wisdom Within

Cover and Interior Design: Derinda Babcock, Deb Haggerty
Editor(s): Peggy Ellis, Judy Hagey, Susan k. Stewart, Deb Haggerty

Author Represented By: WordServe Literary Group, LTD

PUBLISHED BY: Elk Lake Publishing, Inc., 35 Dogwood Drive, Plymouth, MA 02360, 2022

Library Cataloging Data

Names: Barnes, Jean S. Van Dyck and Wrasman, Jessica (Jean S. Van Dyck Barnes and Jessica Wrasman)

Wise Woman Within: Living from the Wisdom Within/ Jean S. Van Dyck Barnes and Jessica Wrasman

222 p. 23cm × 15cm (9 in. × 6 in.)

Identifiers: ISBN-13: 978-1-64949-500-6 (paperback) | 978-1-64949-501-3 (trade paperback) | 978-1-64949-502-0 (e-book)

Key Words: wisdom, multigenerational, healing, friendship, women, self-love, growth mindset

Library of Congress Control Number: 2022938341 Nonfiction

DEDICATION

A new commandment I give to you, that you love one
another: just as I have loved you, you also are to love
one another. (John 13:34)

This book is dedicated to you, dear reader, for having the
courage to undertake this brave work.

TABLE OF CONTENTS

FOREWORD

Years ago, when I felt pulled in a dozen directions by every voice but my own, I landed in a counselor's office.

My goal? To try to figure out how to please everyone in my life.

His goal? To teach me how to say "no" and to find, listen to, and respect my own voice.

I couldn't grasp the concept until he said, "What would the wise woman inside you say to a friend who was struggling with how to please everyone? How would you help her come to a balanced decision?"

I didn't hesitate. I knew exactly what I would advise her, how I would encourage her to consider, first, taking good care of herself then getting to a place of calm and quiet to pray and wait for a variety of answers and responses to surface until one felt right. To "try on" as it were, a variety of solutions until the one that fit her situation best would appear in her mind's eye.

I had good intuition—wise insights from years of study and experiences and from making good choices along with a boatload of mistakes. When I did porch swing chats or kitchen table conversations with other hurting women, I instinctively knew how to guide and question, comfort and assure, and help and encourage.

I had never thought about using this "wise woman within" to guide my own path when I became overwhelmed and confused. When did people-pleasing become my own North Star? This behavior was an auto response from years of living with authority figures who demanded certain responses from me. I had remained stuck in my own mind for decades—a little girl, walking on eggshells trying to care for others.

Imagining wise, older women, who had a balance of caring and confidence, benevolence and boundaries, helped me tremendously. They might have been mentors in my life or authors or famous women—they all had one thing in common: they made a difference in the world without giving too much of themselves away. They had learned to trust their own benevolent wise voice rather than the imaginary voices of criticism and judgment that once whispered doubt into their ears.

What I love about *Wise Woman Within* and the mentoring friendship between two unique women is that beyond telling you how to hear your own wise voice within, their friendship provides dozens of examples of what that looks and feels like in everyday life. They do it with charm, transparency, spiritual depth, psychological balance, love, and humor.

Here's to your journey within these pages and ultimately the journey within your own heart and soul. Finding your own wise voice within is a lot like meeting a dear old friend. She only needs to be recognized, seen, enjoyed, and honored.

What a blessing to have Jean and Jessica as your compassionate traveling companions!

—**Becky Johnson**, *Nourished: A Search for Health, Happiness and a Full Night's Sleep*

PREFACE

For never before in story or rhyme
(not even once upon a time)
has the world ever known you, my friend,
and it never will, not ever again.

—from Nancy Tillman's *On the Night You Were Born*[1]

ACKNOWLEDGMENTS

Michael Van Dyck—We are so thankful for you. Without you, we would not have been able to get our book off the ground. Thank you for believing in us and our message enough to put in so much effort on our behalf.

Greg Johnson—Your willingness to take us on was a gift and a miracle from the Lord. You were so patient with us, and you persevered and fought for our book for nearly three years. We can never repay you.

Becky Johnson—Thank you for your generosity in reading an early version of our text and providing such thoughtful direction for the version presented. We knew you were a kindred spirit when you understood so clearly what we wanted with this book. We thank you for transforming the title to what it is now.

Alan Wild—Thank you for your kindness and generosity in helping us with our many websites and all the technological difficulties we faced.

Deb Haggerty, Susan K. Stewart, and the entire Elk Lake Publishing team—Thank you so much for your partnership and generosity. Peggy Ellis, your edits significantly improved the quality of the work. Thank you for your careful attention to our manuscript.

Katie Chapman—Thank you for reading and improving upon an early draft of our document. Your edits and suggestions transformed our work.

Jess would like to personally thank the following key people:

Andy Wrasman—Thank you for encouraging me every step of the way on this journey. You always believed I could and spoke as if I would.

Tom Choe—Thank you for showing me who Jesus is. Your listening ear, caring heart, and belief in me changed the entire trajectory of my life.

Jen Simmons—Thank you for being a kindred friend and sacred guide. Without you, this book would not have happened. Your words gave me strength and guidance when I needed them most. I'm forever grateful. You are so much a part of this book.

Bethany Lepe—You know how precious your friendship is to me. Thank you for walking with me through it all.

Alison and Gino Landry—Thank you for your years of friendship, your prayer, and your guidance and encouragement along the way.

Bob and Claudia Tremonte—Thank you for your love and for praying over me in our small group days.

Becca Chau—Thank you for your constant support and encouragement, my soul sister. Thank you for believing that I could write.

Linda Lai—Thank you for your friendship, for your prayers, and for your encouragement.

Leah Hardy—Thank you for the beautiful photographs you took early on for this project.

Darcy Leutzow Staddon, Krystin McRoy, and Maame Stephen—Thank you for rallying for me and with me, my sisters in Christ.

Jeff and Donna Horn—The value you placed upon creativity, education, and the church has richly blessed my life. Thank you!

INTRODUCTION

I will instruct you [says the Lord] and teach you in the way you should go; I will counsel you with my loving eye on you. (Psalm 32:8)

A GLIMPSE INTO THE PAST

Last December, our family and friends gathered at Perry's, a trendy restaurant in Larkspur, Marin County, California, to celebrate my son Tom's sixtieth birthday. Searching attics and back corners of cabinets, Haley, my granddaughter, had collected and framed a series of portraits coordinating key events in Tom's life.

Toasting Tom, a friend quipped, "Sixty is the new forty." I countered in jest, "Then the eighties are the new sixties—a hard sell!"

A picture was passed to me, and my mood changed suddenly as I looked at the portrait of an attractive young family. Flooded with memories, I observed a handsome young man with his smiling bride and two adorable preschool-aged sons, clad in their Sunday best. The little boys in matching plaid suit jackets with short pants, their father in a navy suit with white shirt and tie, and the bride in a pale blue classic dress adorned with a string of pearls gave the picture of the perfect family. What a beautiful family, people must have thought. Yet behind the scene, hidden from view, was a young man swallowed by alcoholism which would lead to a divorce, and later, his early death.

The smiling bride was hiding a breaking heart, and the two little boys would grow up without knowing their father.

I was the one pictured in this scene hiding a broken heart.

Sitting at that restaurant in Marin, although fifty-six years had passed and I was far along in the healing process, a wave of sadness flooded over me, only this time there wasn't any pain or anxiety as I felt Jesus embracing me in his arms.

A DIFFERENT PLAN

And we know that for those who love God all things work together for good, for those who are called according to his purpose. (Romans 8:28)

Having two little boys to care and provide for after suffering the loss of my husband, their father, when my boys were so young, propelled me back to teaching, extensive graduate studies, and research. I became mother, father, and breadwinner, provider in every way, for my family—not at all my original plan of having four children and staying at home. God had a different plan for me.

What followed was fifty-eight years as a teacher, counselor, educational psychologist, marriage and family therapist in nine outstanding school districts across the country, and currently a volunteer as a counselor at Saddleback Church in Southern California. God put on my heart the truths of his Scripture, and I was drawn to how psychology and the Bible aligned. This led to pioneering and implementing programs where parents and teachers work together toward the child's cognitive and social development, a model which is now commonly used in schools.

The personal transformation I experienced in my own life motivated me to share my story, research, and five decades of work in the world of psychology, hoping my experiences encourage and motivate others to stir their soul and find healing and strength as I did to become my true self—the person God created and gifted me to be. This process is ongoing this side of heaven, and will be fully realized when, one day, I will see Jesus face-to-face.

In this book, I share insights not only as an educator and psychologist but also as a mom and grandmother who has been divorced, single, and a widow.

This is what I know from having my life and heart transformed as I've come to know the person of Jesus more closely with age. What I know at eighty-five, coming now to the dusk of my days, I hope to pass to you. May the flickering light of truth be passed to you as if my candlestick might dip to light yours, illuminating a path a little brighter, a little clearer for you and yours while undertaking this brave and fierce work of finding the "Wise Woman Within" (WWW). This path leads to knowing Jesus, and to knowing and living your truest authentic identity. (Jean S. Van Dyck Barnes, ME)

—CHAPTER ONE—
WISDOM OBSERVED

HOW JEAN AND I (JESS) FIRST MET

When I first met Jean in the fall of 2017 at Community Bible Study (CBS), I was immediately drawn to her enthusiasm for life and people. This zeal was apparent in her ability to really see people and get straight to the heart of where someone was and sit right there with them. Possessing the abilities to speak profoundly and listen well is rare. For Jean, mastery of both skills is simply who she is. I noticed she possessed the combination of a beautiful, God-given confidence coupled with a fun, self-deprecating sense of humor, and she didn't sweat the small stuff. Most of all, she was strikingly honest and willing to share in ways that would light a path for others, completely without pretense or pretending to be perfect.

When Jean spoke, everyone stopped. If the group was stumped on a question or hesitating for further insight, they would turn to Jean and ask, "Jean, what wisdom can you share on this?" As the newcomer to CBS, I later learned many of these women had had the privilege of knowing Jean for decades, and their respect for her came from observing the way she lived her life through incredible trials. They observed as she cared for her dying husband and as she published her book *Purposeful Parenting: Six Steps to Bring Out the Best in Your Kid*.[1]

This was someone I wanted to be around, someone I wanted to emulate. Early on, when I learned she was, at that time, eighty-four years old, I was surprised she wasn't in her early seventies because of her vitality. That is the attitude and demeanor I want to have when I'm that age. What followed was a friendship and connection that birthed this book—of recognizing the journey we each had and were traveling, of seeking Christ and wholeness—that drew us to each other. Many lattes, laughs, talks, long conversations over yogurt and berries and blue Italian plates of chicken salad later, we had the outline of our book intact. A cross country move for me meant we would work three more years remotely on this book until its completion in 2021.

Too many people face life with many masks which, with time, overtake them. I found it refreshing to meet someone in her eighties, who has become more refined from struggles rather than bogged down and crotchety or victimized or reclusive with false perfectionism. Someone who has both a teachable spirit and childlike wonder, a strong sense of self and room to extend herself to others, and is truly beautiful and truly authentic. Jean has an extensive and impressive background in psychology and education. I can listen to her speak for hours. I glean wonderful wisdom and amazing one-liners like, "You don't have to go the country mile for everyone." The simple and profound way she lives her life impresses me most.

In working closely with Jean on this book project for more than three years, my fondness for her has grown as I see the positive relationships she has with everyone in her life. I've observed regular interactions between Jean and her neighbors, her close friends, in conversations with her sons and grandchildren, with maintenance workers, and in her business dealings. I notice her heart for people and her spirit of getting along with others well in a genuine way. She respects and shows others dignity and love, and that they are cared for. Her life exemplifies the qualities discussed in Scripture from Romans 12:16–17, which says, "Live in harmony with one another. Do not be haughty, but associate with the lowly. Never be wise in your own sight. Repay no one evil for evil, but give thought to do what is honorable in the sight of all."

I became passionate about this project because of Jean's wisdom. I wanted to be a part of putting her knowledge and life experience to print, bringing parts of her testimony and her wisdom to the masses. Finding someone well into their eighties who lives in a way that says, "There is still important work for me to do, and I am excited to do it," was inspirational. God's love for her and her worth spills over to others in a natural way. This is the truth for all of us, in all our days here on earth—we are beloved and needed from birth to death, and yet few blessed with old age have the courage to live each day anticipating God's growth for them. In this case, that growth was beginning a new book endeavor and risking opening her heart to a new relationship in working closely with me. This showed an attractive open-heartedness and freshness of spirit.

Now, as we come to the conclusion of this book journey, having worked through great joys as well as difficulties and differences with choices regarding the book for nearly five years, our fondness for each other remains steadfast, as first sisters in Christ and friends, and then coauthors on this project.

Jean has lived this journey of wisdom, refining it over decades, and the positive aspects of her life well-lived are evident, every day, in her relationships which are real and therefore hard and messy. She makes the journey look easy, living with grace and poise, fun and strength, her transparent openness telling you how God led her through tumultuous days. Thank you, Jean, for your authenticity—the greatest gift to me and a gift to so many.

JEAN MEETS JESS

On September 12, 2017, there was excitement in the air as Community Bible Study (CBS) kicked off the study of the Gospel of Matthew and new core groups gathered. We all knew these relationships formed over the year would impact our lives forever as we shared our faith and love of Jesus, insights and discernments, trials, troubles, and testimonies, growing in love for God and each other. Jess presented a statuesque figure with brightly colored fabric flowing around her as she walked. Her smile lit up her face. Although a beautiful young lady, what drew me to Jess was not her appearance but her honest and transparent manner. Jess was vulnerable as she shared her past frustration and dissatisfaction with her early marriage and career. Not liking the person who she was becoming, Jess sought therapy with a Christian counselor. Following a year of intensive therapy, she realized neither her husband nor her career was the problem, but rather issues from her childhood. Wow, Jess was ahead of the game, having this level of insight and emotional maturity at the tender age of, at that time, thirty-two.

I quickly realized Jess has a strong, mature faith in the Father and Jesus, and extensive knowledge and belief in the Bible. Without direction from others, she had the wisdom to select a Christian college. Upon arriving at college, Jess had the maturity and courage to seek Christian counseling, doing the difficult work of uncovering one's true self from the rubble of the past. The process continues today as Jess lives her belief that godly counsel is "one of the healthiest gifts we can give ourselves."

In my prayer life during this period, I felt God nudging me to write another book. During my morning quiet time with God, I sensed a gentle whisper, "You are hiding my glory." I knew what this meant, having not included in my first book the miracles Jesus had worked in my marriage and the importance of a Christian marriage in family foundations. Looking back, I realized the first draft of my book, *Purposeful Parenting*, had contained several chapters concerning marriage that had been cut in a marketing decision to keep the focus on parenting. Being in my eighties, I prayed to God that, if he wanted me to write, would he please bring someone to help me.

This endeavor happened during a January brunch day when the discussion question was, what are your dreams and goals for the future? Jess, her precious new bundle, Rocky, nestled in her arms, shared she had always wanted to write a book, and now home, and not working as a teacher anymore, she was thinking of how to carve out some writing time. Later, I shared how God was nudging me to write about marriage, and I was praying for a writing partner. In the following days, Jess and I put our heads together, and the ideas in *Wise Woman Within* emerged.

As Jess and I worked together, I witnessed the love, tender care, delight, and creativity Jess lavishes on Bella and Rocky. Three-year-old Bella, already a budding botanist, was fascinated with every flower and plant. Clearly, her parents have demonstrated an appreciation for nature, encouraging her interest in exploring and examining. Rocky, a determined little guy exploring his environment, learned to crawl and stand early with Jess delighting in his every effort. Parenting is a seven-days-a-week and twenty-four-hours-a-day assignment, so Jess is also open and transparent regarding the frustrations and exhaustion all parents experience. However, she is always willing to pick herself up and continue to try to be the best mother and wife she can be.

Since Jess and I began working on this project, our relationship has deepened as we've laughed and lamented, lingering over convictions and choices. Our friendship has many faces—confidante, counselor, critic, daughter, friend, prayer partner, but most of all delight and love as we share the stories of WWW.

Our goal is for you to exchange a life of striving, stressing, and surviving for the joy, peace, and love only God can give. Discard your false selves and be the true person God created. See yourself as God sees you, created in his image. Each one of us is a unique masterpiece with a unique purpose. As Scripture tells us, "For you formed my inward parts; you knitted me together in my mother's womb. I praise you, for I am fearfully and wonderfully made. Wonderful are your works; my soul knows it very well. My frame was not hidden from you, when I was being made in secret, intricately woven in the depths of the earth" (Psalm 139:13-15). The days of our life were planned before our conception. Knowing this, we can trust and embrace our story as it unfolds, since the unknown parts belong to a God who knows all the parts.

By owning your own unique story—the good, bad, and ugly—you gradually learn to live your true authentic self. As Brené Brown wrote, "You either walk into your story and own your truth, or you live outside of your story, hustling for your worthiness."[2] This transition will last a lifetime as you surrender everything and everyone to the loving hands of Jesus. With Jesus at the center, anxiety and worry subside as joy and peace reign.

PRACTICES TO PONDER

1. Is there something specific that spoke to you regarding what we shared?
2. Among your friends or church members, is there a mature Christian who could be a suitable mentor?
3. Do you have a teachable spirit and desire to grow spiritually?

PRAYER

For I know the plans I have for you, declares the LORD, plans for welfare and not for evil, to give you a future and a hope. Then you will call upon me and come and pray to me, and I will hear you. You will seek me and find me, when you seek me with all your heart. I will be found by you, declares the LORD, and I will restore your fortunes and gather you from all the nations and all the places where I have driven you, declares the LORD, and I will bring you back to the place from which I sent you into exile. (Jeremiah 29:11–14)

—CHAPTER TWO—
THE TRUE SELF

For who has understood the mind of the Lord so as to instruct him?' But we have the mind of Christ." (1 Corinthians 2:16)

She is spiritually discerning and intuitive because Christ has revealed his freedom to her; the freedom spoken of in 1 Corinthians 2. She is not wise of the world, but wise in the discernment of God.

BECOMING YOUR TRUEST SELF—JEAN

Let's look at the Wise Woman Within (WWW). Most apparent is her open, transparent way of relating with others. A deep security upholds her from a place of profound belonging that guides her life. She knows how deeply loved she is, how cared for, and how crafted even before she knew herself. Because of this inner knowledge of her worth, she refuses to be bound by feelings of shame and fear. She can share openly, and she knows what belongs to her and what is not hers to carry. She is not a people pleaser, but instead, she lives to please the Lord.

Unjumbling the WWW requires a deep look inside as the authentic self emerges.

Reaching the point of consistent authenticity comes from confidence rooted in knowing one's preciousness as a child of God, firmly planted in his kingdom. Out of this belonging stirs the excitement of actively becoming the person God created you to be now, and will continue into eternity.

We are God's masterpieces—created in God's image with unique talents and abilities, personalities, experiences, and passions. Ephesians tells us, "For we are his workmanship, created in Christ Jesus for good works, which God prepared beforehand, that we should walk in them" (2:10).

When living out of the true self, you appear on the outside to others as you truly are in your innermost being. You feel good about yourself as you truly are. You are practicing rather than simply professing your values, keeping your promises, and holding yourself accountable. You are purposeful and intent on doing your best, transparent enough that even when you make a mistake, you own it, letting others see your heart to make things right.

In parenting, such openness and vulnerability strengthen credibility as children see their parent loves them enough to trust them with the truth, circles back around to check in, and asks for forgiveness when needed. Letting your children see you care about virtue and integrity, and you yourself are continually growing, helps them see how to do that themselves.

Being your true self is a daily practice demanding integrity and interdependence with one's creator. This path cannot be walked alone, but hand in hand, moment-by-moment with Jesus. Life is messy and so are we, yet the knowledge of an identity rooted in Christ allows the Wise Woman Within to stand on solid ground in the middle of life's many difficulties. Psalm 73 tells us, "Nevertheless, I am continually with you; you hold my right hand. You guide me with your counsel, and afterward you will receive me to glory" (vv. 23–24). This is the path to loving ourselves and loving each other.

William Shakespeare in *Hamlet* addresses this practice of being true to yourself. "To thine own self be true."[1] I (Jean) remember my mother reciting this old saying, instructing me to never lie to my mother, or to others, or to myself.

WHO WE REALLY ARE

Brené Brown, author of *The Gifts of Imperfection,*[2] writes, "Authenticity is the daily practice of letting go of who we think we are supposed to be and embracing who we actually are." Choosing authenticity means cultivating the ability to be imperfect, allowing ourselves to be vulnerable, and setting boundaries. As a researcher, Brown shares with her students the practice of choosing "discomfort over discontent" to enhance authenticity. For example, fear may feel uncomfortable when it arises, and to avoid discomfort, we distract ourselves or reject our feelings and needs, but ultimately, this is never satisfying. Not honoring our true feelings and needs forces them to leak out when we least expect it, harming ourselves and others. How much better to experience struggle due to growth in pursuing a path to our true selves instead of stagnation or resistance to truth or change.

Becoming your truest authentic self is a long, sometimes painful process requiring introspection and counsel as you unpack the masks you wear which hide who you truly are. Everyone has a false self, constructed to avoid rejection and to win approval. Maintaining a false self requires pretending and lying while being authentic requires the truth. To uncover your authentic Wise Woman Within requires a deeper look at patterns in your family of origin and wounds inflicted by those you love and trust. In the process of inner exploration with God's guidance, we grow, heal, and love ourselves more truly for who we are. We begin to embrace our true selves and find joy in being who God intended us to be. We can then understand the depth of our need for a Savior, fully appreciating the extent of his love.

I am compelled to live honestly and authentically, regardless of my past because Father God, maker of heaven and earth, called and knows me by name, and has a plan for my future. Looking to the future with hope, I am urged to live with my whole heart and to extend the love first extended to me to others

PRACTICES TO PONDER

1. What external or internal stress or storm might be a sign that something is not right spiritually?

2. How might staying "busy" be blocking you from listening to and spending time with God?

3. What anxieties and worries are upsetting you today?

PRAYER

Father, I surrender to you today my striving, scheming, manipulating, and spinning half-truths to those around me to build myself up. I invite you to teach me your ways and to come into my heart that I may live in dependence on you, Jesus, my Lord and Savior.

—CHAPTER THREE—
THE VOICE OF WISDOM

And rising very early in the morning, while it was still dark, he departed and went out to a desolate place, and there he prayed. (Mark 1:35)

OUR MODEL

Jesus is the perfect model of an authentic self and source of all wisdom. As John Eldredge wrote, "Jesus is simply himself. Playful, cunning, generous, fierce—not one moment is contrived. Jesus never plays to the audience, never kowtows to the opposition, never takes his cues from the circus around him. He is simply himself."[1] No false selves or false faces, just simply himself.

A favorite image of mine found frequently in Psalms and Isaiah is God taking me by the hand. Jesus, ever loving and kind, walking with the crowds gathering around him, laughing, hugging, teaching, and healing. Jesus celebrating at weddings, even creating the best wine ever tasted, eating and drinking with tax collectors, and cuddling children on his lap.

Jesus was totally committed and obedient in following his Father's purpose for his life. God's will was the center of his life, and time alone with the Father was essential. We see this in the Bible when Jesus leaves his disciples and goes alone on the mountainside to pray. In the Garden of

Gethsemane, when sorrow overwhelmed Jesus, he prayed, "My Father, if this cannot pass unless I drink it, your will be done" (Matthew 26:42).

Our primary task is giving up the selfish self and placing God at the center of our lives. Jesus taught us: "Love the Lord your God with all your heart and with all your soul and with all your mind. This is the great and first commandment. And a second is like it: 'You shall love your neighbor as yourself'" (Matthew 22:37–39). The only way to follow the Great Commandment is to place God at the center, guiding your thoughts. Failure to commit and focus on Jesus causes us to place someone or something at the center to fill the void.

Distorted thinking dims our view of who God made us to be, leading us to become god of our own lives. Like Jesus, calmly differentiating our authentic true self from surrounding voices, and discerning the purpose God has uniquely prepared for us, gives us great strength as our core comfort comes from the creator rather than our circumstances. God and Jesus are one. Only in this alignment with God, realizing his love for us, and in understanding who he created us to be, can we fully love with our whole hearts. We accomplish this by following the model Jesus lives out—spending time alone in the presence of God. Jesus walked, moment by moment, in the power of the Holy Spirit.

Peter Scazerro, author of *Emotionally Healthy Spirituality* commented, "Jesus modeled contentment amidst pressure, calmness in the face of betrayal, and power to forgive at his crucifixion—the fruit of a long history of living in knowing deeply that he was 'beloved' by his Father."[2] Why do many of us lack the qualities Jesus modeled? Scazzero believes our busy lives cause us to skim over our relationship with God, not giving him the time necessary to develop faith that shines through us.

INTIMACY WITH GOD

When we turn to God seeking to know him, the veil gradually lifts. As our relationship deepens, we begin to take on some of his glory. "And we all, with unveiled face, beholding the glory of the Lord, are being transformed into the same image from one degree of glory to another. For this comes from the Lord who is the Spirit" (2 Corinthians 3:18).

According to Oswald Chamber's daily devotional, *My Utmost for His Highest,*

> The greatest characteristic a Christian can exhibit is this completely unveiled openness before God, which allows that person's life to become a mirror for others. When the Spirit fills us, we are transformed, and by beholding God we become mirrors ... The most important rule for us is to concentrate on keeping our lives open to God. Let everything else including work, clothes, and food be set aside. The busyness of daily life and being overly scheduled obscures our concentration on God. Never let a hurried lifestyle disturb the relationship of abiding in him. This is an easy thing to allow, so we must guard against busyness. The most difficult lesson of the Christian life is learning to continue beholding as in a mirror the glory of God.[3]

As in any close relationship, intimacy and love grow through openness and honesty—sharing vulnerabilities. God wants an intimate loving relationship with us. We can trust God with our deepest hurts. He will comfort and provide for us.

When we seek a deeper relationship with Jesus, our prayers will flow from a heart and soul experiencing a full range of emotions. God handles our emotions but also encourages us to bring them to him. David, who God said was a man after his own heart, expressed the full range of emotions while writing the Psalms, from the depths of depression and regret to the highest peaks of joy and victory. We can turn to these Psalms—prayers of empathy—knowing this imperfect man, whom God loved so much, feels what we feel. They show us a raw heart focused on God, yet another way our lives are intricately, intimately woven together with Christ.

An important part of transformation is experiencing the discomfort that accompanies realization and openness. Often giving up something or confronting "deaths" of all kinds in this life—of expectations, a future we had decided for ourselves—is necessary to experience God's resurrections in our daily life. Emotional growth is the same—pride must die for humility and empathy to grow in its place. The process of transition associated with giving up anything is often uncomfortable, perhaps simply because it involves uncharted action. New is scary. We must readjust to embrace the "now."

Living authentically also involves connecting with others without letting them determine your behaviors. Jesus, staying calm while seeing our sins clearly, refrains from criticism, and instead speaks truth with resolve.

TURNING THE SPOTLIGHT

The story of Jesus talking to the Samaritan woman at the well is familiar. Jesus asks her for a drink of water: "The woman said to him, 'Sir, you have nothing to draw water with, and the well is deep. Where do you get that living water?'" (John 4:11). In response, Jesus shares he could give her "living water" that would well up to eternal life.

Jesus gently turns the spotlight on the deep well of hurt and pain within the Samaritan woman's heart, noting she has had five husbands and the current guy she is living with is not her husband. The Samaritan woman changes the subject to the coming Messiah who will explain everything. Jesus declared, "I who speak to you am he" (John 4:26).

Jesus was not reactive or judgmental. He turned the spotlight on the woman and offered the Spirit, truth, and a way forward. In other words, Jesus offered, as he does for all, repentance and restoration all wrapped in love. The woman was transformed, and the truth became contagious as well. Her testimony compelled many Samaritans from the village to become believers. The same opportunity awaits all of us who are willing and open to have such a shared legacy.

INTEGRITY FROM GOD'S PERSPECTIVE

In Psalm 15, David asks God who can live in his "sacred tent." The answer he receives is, "He who walks blamelessly and does what is right and speaks truth in his heart" (v. 2).

Jesus always spoke the truth. "I am the way, and the truth, and the life. No one comes to the Father except through me" (John 14:6). Even when honesty was costly or confrontational, Jesus never veered from it. Conversely, lying defines Satan who Jesus called the father of lies. As God, Jesus is unable to lie, for his very being is truth.

JESUS AS OUR EMOTIONAL EXAMPLE

It seems people who don't spend time in the Word often think of Jesus as perpetually happy and gentle, without any passionate feelings, akin to Mr. Rogers asking, "Won't you be my neighbor?" with legs crossed and voice chipper. But stop and think about the weight of the love and compassion, distress, rejection, and oppression he faced from birth to the end of his human life—is there anyone who has felt more than Jesus? Yet, having felt the full scope of human emotions that we too feel, he focuses in on and lives out his God-given purpose with clarity and healthy boundaries.

Jesus feels and expresses his emotions. Created in God's image, we too need to master and understand healthy expression of emotions. When I operate in the power of the Holy Spirit, kindness and compassion flow through me naturally. Conversely, pride takes over as soon as my selfish self sprouts feelings of anger, greed, and jealousy. The Holy Spirit gets snuffed out, and the false self begins spinning half-truths and lies.

Jesus shows us another way to navigate tense moments. When Jesus healed the man with the crippled hand on the Sabbath, he looked around at the crowd "with anger, grieved at their hardness of heart" (Mark 3:5). However, he continued to heal the man's hand. Even in his distress, he focused on his overall mission and responded without reacting. He had enough emotional currency saved up from his time with the Father that he remained true to his passion and purpose, and executed his vision in the face of the smallest to the most heinous adversity.

Based on a loving union with his Father, Jesus recognized his worth and value. Jesus was all about relationships. After all, he commanded us to love others as ourselves. Jesus had friends, worked cooperatively with others, and was consistently truly himself. He experienced and expressed a full range of emotions as a teacher, mentor, healer, and Savior. He was kind, compassionate, and delighted in people. He sacrificed his life on the cross to pay our sin debt. His life is a passionate love letter to humanity—to be held and read over again—of suffering for all so all who receive Him not forever suffer.

PRACTICES TO PONDER

1. How can you begin to see Jesus in the people you encounter today?

2. What might be one way you can let go of power and control while choosing to love and serve someone today?

3. Is there anything you need to give up or let die so something else might grow in its place?

Ask God to put someone on your heart to whom you can extend kindness and compassion.

PRAYER

Let love be genuine. Abhor what is evil; hold fast to what is good. Love one another with brotherly affection. Outdo one another in showing honor. (Romans 12:9–10)

—CHAPTER FOUR—
THE ORIGINAL FALSE SELF

Then the eyes of both were opened, and they knew that
they were naked. And they sewed fig leaves together
and made themselves loincloths. (Genesis 3:7)

ORIGINAL AUTHENTICITY IN EDEN

We know the story. Two people stood in perfect
partnership and union with each other in marriage and with
their creator—man and woman, the first people knowing
only good, enjoying community with God and each other,
protected and provided for all their days without sorrow
and worry. This is the picture of original authenticity—
enjoying one's life and one's creator, for always.

This was perfection—openness and vulnerability in their
relationships without shame or feelings of inadequacy.
Adam and Eve felt good about themselves and their bodies.
They were naked and felt no shame. Every deep human
passion and drive is deeply rooted in this archetypal
ancestral desire.

While evil was present, they were unable to see it because
God protected them. "Do not go there," God said, as a good
and loving father. It was never about the forbidden fruit but
the forbidden rejection of God's way, the rejection of his plan.
What was his plan? Joy and community with people in his

stunning creation and with lavish provision in perfect unity. He wanted his beloved creation, his children, to experience only the best, for their enjoyment and his own.

In opposition to God's command, Eve ate the fruit, but also encouraged Adam to do the same. Instantly their eyes opened, and they realized they were naked. Flooded with fear and anxiety, newly aware of the weight of shame, they sewed fig leaves together in an attempt to ease their humiliation for what they had done and their self-consciousness. They felt a new insecurity in their relations with God, the loss of protection causing fear, anxiety, and shame. Their once-perfect relationship with each other became conflictual and insecure.

The result of this seemingly "small" act of disobedience reminds us there is no small sin. All acts of sin have consequence.

FIG LEAVES—THE FIRST FALSE SELF.

Adam and Eve took the quickest, largest coverings they could find and, still feeling shameful, did the only thing left to do—they hid. In this portrait of human history, we see the first attempt by people to avoid facing the truth. When confronted by God, the first signs of emotional dysfunction emerged. Adam and Eve began transferring blame, neither taking responsibility for their own actions.

Satan was satisfied as he had sown the seed of mistrust and tempted Adam and Eve to take control and be god of their own lives. The lie propagated by the Evil One, which flourishes and is so prevalent today, is that you don't need to trust God—just take control, become god of your own life. This lie led to pride, the sin which threw Satan down from heaven. Pride always results in the idol of "I"—the worship of self as god, with the desired omnipotence and omniscience therein.

God has always had firm boundaries. Out of his desire to protect the healthy and good, he guarded Adam and Eve from the garden by sending them out, blocking the gate entry with flames and preventing reentry until the situation was resolved. What a great and gracious God—understanding the entire picture and remaining redemption-minded.

GOD'S PLAN OF REDEMPTION

God immediately took pity on Adam and Eve's shameful state and provided a solution. He saw their pathetic bodily masks (the fig leaves) and made garments of skin for Adam and his wife, covering them with greater fur clothing (Genesis 3:21), which I imagine was warmer and more comfortable than wearing leaves. Mink underwear. Not only did God immediately comfort his people in a practical way, but he also gave them a symbol, foreshadowing what was and is to come. This first blood animal sacrifice was required to physically warm and cover them, demonstrating not only that death had entered the world, but also foreshadowing the coming blood sacrifice that would redeem it. Jesus's sacrifice—death amidst perfect sinlessness—would allow them to revert to their original state of authenticity. The blood of God in human form would be shed for a people set against God, remuneration for returning to the eternal presence of a good God—humanity's covering for salvation always.

Adam and Eve could have rejected the second covering, refusing to remove their fig leaves to stand in the truth of their shame before God, but they didn't. There is an important moment to consider between wearing their own fig leaves, which had failed them, and God's coverings, which provided recognition and healing. To put one on, they had to take the other off, leaving them fully exposed before themselves, before each other, and before God. They had to come out of their hiding, disrobing their false self, to embrace who they truly are and what they had done before their Father, themselves, and one another. Standing in and absorbing the pain of the truth, they would have to feel every part of it and acknowledge what had gone wrong. Thus, pain also entered God's good world before human death. Standing exposed, their nakedness was not only of body, but of heart, mind, spirit, their words—their entire being.

Shedding their leaves and receiving better coverings designed by God himself is physical representation of the spiritual significance and implications of their choices on their eternal position of authenticity before their Father in heaven. They learned the first lesson in going awry— that a lack of alignment with God leads to devastation and disunity with oneself, causing the desire to hide and mask.

Our choice is the same. We can stay under the tree of shame, in a continual fog of busyness and denial, masking the pain of awareness and truth. In that case, we miss the forest for the trees. Or we can embrace the freedom God has for us by exposing our pain, shame, and truth before him continually. Exposure invites healing and life. In our willingness to see and feel, we venture into all the freedom God has for us, knowing we are not to live out of the laser pinpoint of real failure, but in the dwelling of God's covering and a knowledge of him. This changes everything. This covering says, "I am" and so "you are." I am Christ, and so you are free and saved from yourself.

Practices to Ponder

1. Ask God to open your eyes to lies you believe that prevent you from healing and growing.

2. Has there been a time when you were closer to God? What drew you away?

3. How might you change today if you stop looking for human approval and seek only the approval of God?

Prayer

Lord Jesus, help me to be transparent before you that I might find the love and acceptance you have for me. Remind me that you love me completely as I am. Teach me to love myself and others as you love. Please send me a kindred friend who might get to know me and whom I can get to know, so we can be witnesses of your love to each other. Amen.

> "For God so loved the world, that he gave his only Son, that whoever believes in him should not perish but have eternal life" (John 3:16).

—CHAPTER FIVE—
THE FALSE SELF GROWS

The unexamined life is not worth living.—Socrates

But if you have bitter jealousy and selfish ambition in your hearts, do not boast and be false to the truth. This is not the wisdom that comes down from above, but is earthly, unspiritual, demonic. For where jealousy and selfish ambition exist, there will be disorder and every vile practice. (James 3:14–16)

DISTORTED REALITY

Most of us live with a distorted view of reality. The choice is to defend the distortion or to challenge it. Initially, facing the distortion may seem more painful, but in the long run, it is less painful than living in denial, living a lie. The truth will eventually surface. The longer the denial, the harsher the reality. The deep digging process requires a commitment to continually learn and the willingness to hold oneself accountable.

You can't resolve problems by hiding from them, living in a fog of drugs or a fervor of activity. You are much more likely to resolve problems by recognizing them explicitly, thinking about them clearly, and praying about them unceasingly. The process of becoming a new creation begins by replacing old thoughts, feelings, and habits with God's truth.

When faced with a dilemma, we have a choice—recycle or resolve. The longer we recycle our problems the bigger the mess when we finally attempt to resolve them. Before tragedy strikes, God always erects caution signs along the way warning us of trouble ahead. Avoiding facing the pain inherent in unearthing the truth is human of all of us. However, when we continue to deny the truth, we choose to take the low road. By sticking with our own makeshift fig leaves, when God may have something better, we obstruct God's progress in making us new creations.

In his book, *Life Mapping*, author John Trent, PhD, discusses authentic living as compared to image management. He says image management is trying to keep up a false self while not dealing with private issues, which ultimately creates tension until there is a breakdown in values[1] An image manager compromises the truth and integrity to keep the image intact. Objective reality flees. Deception rules. This practice of lying and keeping appearances while covering up corruption is listed as one of the "seven woes" in the Bible—a sure way to guarantee God's anger.

According to Trent, the antidote to image management is authentic living. This requires the humility to take an honest look inside. The commitment to continually learning. The willingness to hold yourself accountable. The more we live as authentic selves, the happier and healthier we will be. Initiating the adventure of authentic living takes incredible courage and resolve.

Nowhere is seeking the truth more important than in family relationships. Since birth, our minds have been programmed by our experiences and education. Some of it was good, but we may have developed thought patterns that hampered our growth because they are not based on the truth. We must uncover behavior patterns learned as a child that are now preventing us from being who God created us to be. These can be behaviors that prevent us from enjoying loving, intimate relations, or prevent us from using our abilities for his purpose.

We all get our sense of self-worth from our family of origin. If we take a deep look inside to examine our thoughts, feelings, and behaviors, we may discover dysfunctional patterns that began in childhood as a means of survival and carried into adulthood that prevent a proper perspective. We have all formed defenses which distort reality or built facades to present ourselves as more perfect than others. We have all erected walls to insulate us from pain.

THE FACADE OF PERFECTION

A common pattern is forming a facade of perfection, refusing to recognize imperfections in oneself. Recognizing faults in others, however, is fair game, for it helps one to feel more perfect if surrounded by imperfect others. We all know families who send Christmas letters recounting the highlights of another perfect year in the perfect family with perfect children who lead perfect lives. This is even more prevalent on social media—one perfect glance after another. The only catch—life is not perfect. Life is difficult. Life is messy.

DENIAL

To keep the facade of perfection in place requires a lot of denial. Denial is a key survival skill we all learned early in childhood. It stunted our emotional growth by allowing us to dodge reality and to accept a lie as the truth. Denial protected us from our feelings and helped repress the pain of our family environment. Our shame and guilt caused us to be silent rather than open and honest.

My experience is the greater the need to be perfect on the outside, the greater the need to repress what is happening internally. Denial hinders us from developing into emotionally healthy adults. In the process of self-discovery, we begin to realize the role denial played in our lives, forming the basis for accepting the truth of our family history. Proverbs speaks to this in chapter 3: "Do not forget my teaching ... It will be healing to your flesh and refreshment to your bones" (vv. 1–8).

CRITICISM

If parents emphasize too strongly the need to be perfect, or are overly critical, children begin to associate being loved with not making mistakes. The shame and guilt are so strong that, if they discover themselves to be less than perfect, children will deny reality to avoid the pain. Parents who have a tendency toward perfectionism need to be especially aware of this being passed on to their children, instead sending the message that making mistakes is a necessary part of life. We often learn more from our mistakes than from our triumphs.

PITFALLS OF PEOPLE-PLEASING, PERFECTIONISM, AND POSSESSIONS

People-pleasing is a snare that entraps. You become overly concerned about what others think of you. Seeing yourself through the eyes of others is unhealthy. Others' opinions are distorted by their own perceptions of reality. Furthermore, it is impossible to know what they really think about you. When you view yourself from others' perspectives, you add your own distortions to theirs, becoming trapped as you strive to present an acceptable persona.

The need to please people, to pretend to be perfect, and to lie to cover up the truth begins early. I am well acquainted with the practices of perfectionism and people-pleasing, having learned all about these traits in my family of origin.

My (Jean's) beautiful, charming mother had an explosive temper. At her worst, she would throw things. She'd scream. She once threw my brother's coat at him with his belt attached. She also threw my record collection at me. My mom's rage episodes and resulting behaviors needed to be addressed as I matured.

As a child, I quickly learned how to please my mother. On the plus side, I became a good cook and skilled at household tasks while in elementary school. On the downside, I developed a fear of anger and became a people-pleaser and peace-at-any-cost type of gal. A psychologist in training, I practiced judging my mom's moods, warding off gathering signs of impending trouble. This breeds a false self that believes, "I am what other people think."

I carried these skills into my marriage. Shortly after the birth of my first son, my husband began drinking heavily, spending money we didn't have, cracking up cars, and staying out until three or four in the morning. I prayed and prayed, sought the help of relatives and clergy, and eventually found myself screaming at him just like my mom. I realized I needed to learn healthy expressions of anger. Following a divorce, numerous courses in psychology, and counseling, I learned to express my thoughts and feelings in a straightforward and candid manner.

I learned anger is a fact of life. Attacking others or exploding is not necessary to discuss what makes you feel angry, and sarcasm is not healthy expression of anger either. Realizing this was the first step in uncovering my true self, beginning to chip away at my perfectionism and people pleasing.

Love of Money

> For the love of money is a root of all kinds of evils. It
> is through this craving that some have wandered away
> from the faith and pierced themselves with many pangs.
> (1 Timothy 6:10)

Money can be another obstacle thwarting one's true self. Leo Tolstoy's parable "How Much Land Does a Man Need"[2] is an excellent allegory which brilliantly depicts this biblical principle. The parable tells the story of a man, Pahom, who learns of a simple-minded group of people called the Bashkirs who own a huge plot of land. He goes to them and begins to negotiate to purchase some of their land. The Bashkirs make an interesting proposition: for a small sum of a thousand rubles (the equivalent of fifteen US dollars), they agree they will allow him to keep whatever amount of land Pahom can walk around and mark off with his shovel from daybreak to sunset. He must return to his starting point before the sun sets. If, however, he does not reach his starting point by the end of the day, he will lose the rubles and receive no land.

Pahom agrees and takes off at the start of the day with an audience of Baskirs nearby. He reaches a point far from where he began toward the close of the day and begins to panic. Thinking he will not be able to return to his starting point, he begins shedding all his clothing, running faster to get back before dusk. After pushing himself to the extreme to acquire as much as he possibly can, he drops down at the starting point having reached his destination. The only problem is that when his servants approach him to help him, they find he has died.

Thus, the story's ending answers the title's proposed question with the statement, "Six feet from his head to his heels was all he needed." Just six feet, from his head to his feet was all the land he ultimately needed and acquired—the space he occupied while living and the space he would take up in the ground upon his death.

This simple yet profound story depicts the temptation to trade our earthly lives for so little, which the world tells us is so much, at the expense of our soul. In this case, Pahom gave away his life to greed, which left him empty. The "simple-minded" people knew Pahom's greed would kill him and were the wise ones in the end.

This is often how Satan works, as he did in the beginning and as he did when Tolstoy published the story in 1886. Though we have what is sufficient, the desire for "the other" or for a little more, might keep us poor and indebted in spirit. If we're not careful, desire can lead to a life of misery, a life of spiritual poverty. The original temptation is "I have all this, but if only I had just a little bit more." This struggle can misdirect our lives so easily today. This struggle creates falsehoods and distorts the true self. If we are to become wise, we must become like-minded with Christ by placing paramount importance on matters of the heart rather than external matters. As in the words of 1 Samuel 16:7, "Man looks on the outward appearance, but the LORD looks on the heart."

As wise women, we too need to concern ourselves with matters of the heart. We must come to the place where we know deeply and feel the love of God is better than all we strive for, and we already possess this deep love. We must daily take the time to sit in and feel this love and make it our number one priority.

SOCIETY TODAY AND MONEY

Do not love the world or the things in the world. If anyone loves the world, the love of the Father is not in him. For all that is in the world—the desires of the flesh and the desires of the eyes and pride of life—is not from the Father but is from the world. And the world is passing away along with its desires, but whoever does the will of God abides forever. (1 John 2:15–17)

Our society is in love with money and all the trappings money can buy. God is not. God tells us to love people not possessions.

Living in Orange County, California, one is constantly confronted with materialism. All around is the overarching cloud of belligerent striving for a house with all the bells and whistles, a flashy car, and a designer wardrobe. We are all guilty, me included. However, when possessions or money define who we are, then fear of loss takes over. Insatiable greed takes over. Money becomes our security rather than God.

We use people when we love stuff. We use stuff when we love people. The false self believes "I am what I have." The true self believes "I am complete in who God made me to be." Our focus shifts from striving and grasping for more to looking to our creator, recognizing the beauty of what is, and seeing that the majesty of God is enough. Christian author and artist Ruth Chou Simons articulately sums up this problem in her devotional book *Gracelaced* when she writes, "Any notion I have of finding comfort and satisfaction in the perfection of my surroundings has simply shown itself for what it is: an idol of the heart that can neither sustain nor deliver."[3]

THE PERFORMANCE TRAP

Related to striving for money is the performance trap. We desire our children perform so they may one day have enough, perhaps more than we have, or they might maintain an image that makes us comfortable. As a parent and an educator, I realize it is easy for kids to fall into the performance trap both at home and at school. As a parent, I was into raising good boys, good students, and good athletes. At school, the focus was good behavior, good grades, and being smart. The grading process instills the concepts of perfectionism, and, for many, the goal is to achieve straight A's. We've lost sight of God's design of enjoying his creation, gaining understanding and wisdom, which is an end unto itself, finding application to life, and contributing to society and the welfare of others. On the game field or playground, athletic prowess and popularity are king—no wonder many kids end up thinking they are not good enough. The false self believes, "I am what I do." Additionally, we begin thinking that life is about completion and earning, rather than growing and enjoying.

A family focus on money and performance digs a chasm between one's understanding of and reliance upon God. It is confusing for kids to try to understand a God who loves them for who they are as a human being and child of God, while at the same time facing daily judgment of what they do and how well they do it, growing up as a human being whose dignity is wrapped up in performance and accolades. We are wise to explain to our children (and to remind ourselves) God does not need our works but loves us as a mother loves her newborn baby. When we grow to do good works, it is through alignment with our good Father, desiring to do what he does—becoming more righteous, to make our world a better place. We want to worship God by living a life that honors him not as a performance or to earn love which is already given, but because it is freeing and good for us to live under his umbrella of goodness.

There is a fine line between living a life worthy of Christ while pursuing one's God-given talents and striving merely for personal gain. We must understand we are nurturing our children's and our own hearts, a far more valuable treasure than anything we might wear or carry. God provides for us—even our talents with which one may earn a living. We cannot switch this understanding and make life a contest of earning. Our focus, either God or money, directs the entire paths of our lives and our children's lives.

CREATED TO BE AUTHENTIC

> Truly, I say to you, unless you turn and become like children, you will never enter the kingdom of heaven. (Matthew 18:3)

When infants are born, they are authentic, they are their true selves. From birth until about seven years of age, children typically remain true to themselves. I have always enjoyed working with young children because they speak their mind and act on their beliefs. They recognize the feelings of those around them and are candid while sharing their reactions. Curiosity abounds. They are keen observers and find joy in every new flower petal and crawling bug. Little ones are trusting and unpretentious, in other words—authentic.

WHY A FALSE SELF?

By third or fourth grade, false selves come into view as kids attempt to cover up their fears concerning an assortment of issues such as not belonging, failure, and not being good enough. They form cliques and begin shedding their true selves to fit in with their friends' view of what is "cool." The goal of the false self is to avoid rejection and win approval. Fear is the driving force leading us to conform, hide, and people-please, unopposed by a lack of courage to show up and be who we are. Behind this fear and hiding is brokenness, in every false self, that needs healing.

Unfortunately, this is not only the condition of school age kids. Each of us, at some point in life, will struggle with feelings of low self-worth or feelings of inferiority.

Failure to obtain the promotion, weight gain, divorce, lack of education or of achievement are just a few of the situations which can discourage us and diminish our self-esteem. We compare ourselves, often unfavorably, to others. This practice of grading ourselves, further agitated by social media, either renders us motionless and defeated, or propels us to a ceaseless path of striving.

To state the condition precisely: Some can't start while others can't stop. Ceaseless striving traps us into thinking we would feel better about ourselves if we tried harder. We all come up losers when we adopt the attitude that we must be better than our neighbor or friend on social media, or that we must win to feel good about ourselves.

LACK OF TRUTH

> Lying lips are an abomination to the LORD, but those who act faithfully are his delight. (Proverbs 12:22)

Sadly, truth is disappearing in today's world. Lies are called the truth, and a truth one wants to disbelieve is rejected as a false truth. On a personal level, we often manipulate the facts, rationalizing we have done nothing wrong. Whether it is little white lies, gossip, exaggeration, or blatant deception, the temptation to fudge on the truth is always waiting to trip us.

Often the reason we lie is to protect our false self. However, the root cause for our lying is the lack of trust in God. Instead of simply obeying him and telling the truth, we attempt to manipulate people's perception of us and in the process, lose what is of utmost value—our integrity and authenticity.

The essence of choice is to practice denial or to acknowledge the truth. It is difficult, however, for most of us to admit our faults and shortcomings, even to God. Humility and honesty are necessary to recognize our weaknesses.

Most of us would rather pretend we are perfect.

Being a perfectionist or people-pleaser is much more than a false self because perfectionism becomes a lifestyle. Consistently striving for an unreachable goal results in deception. Neglecting the truth that only God is perfect, we attempt to dull the pain with addictions. Only when we realize our sin and brokenness can we seek God's healing and begin to discover God's purpose for our lives, giving birth to our true self.

From God's perspective, there are no losers, only sinners who have not turned to him. We are all worthy winners in God's eyes. Each of us has the potential to accomplish whatever he calls us to do.

Self-Awareness

As John Eldredge instructs:

> God is after something critical: he's after what is going on in our heart. When you find yourself lost or disoriented, feeling discontented, it flushes deeper things in the heart. Stuff begins to surface, like all those feelings of abandonment or fear or self-hatred. But, actually, dear friend, that stuff is gold. Because it opens you up to deeper healing, deeper freedom; it opens a door for transformation and restoration. It prepares the way for you to become a more wholehearted human being.[4]

The first step in becoming your authentic self is gaining awareness of your false self. Ask the question, "What version of myself do I most frequently portray or rely on?" Remember, false selves are shields providing protection from shame, fear, or anger, in our attempts to be loved and belong. How are others impacted by your false self? The false self is based on lies or half-truths. Over time, people realize you are not truthful, a realization that prevents true friendship, because your true self never shows up. We can dismantle the false self only by seeking the help and healing power of the Holy Spirit, thereby giving birth to the authentic, integrated self.

DISMANTLING THE FALSE SELF

1. Seek solitude with Jesus. Begin each day thanking and delighting in the Lord, listening for his guidance.
2. Be open and transparent. This requires speaking the truth—no half-truths or false truths—just the facts. Uncover and address destructive behaviors and addictions.
3. Distinguish between feelings and facts before making decisions or taking action.
4. Pursue freedom to live your true self in Christ—broken, humble, truthful, and grateful. Say no to manipulation, set firm boundaries, define what is your responsibility and what belongs to someone else.
5. Wait on the Lord. God is never in a hurry. Many wrong decisions are made by jumping ahead of the Lord as we all recognize in humbling hindsight.
6. Practice a growth mindset by becoming a lifelong learner. Find the courage to explore why you do what you do and change rather than stay stuck in anxiety and guilt.

PRACTICES TO PONDER

1. Can you identify your false self?

2. What "fig leaf" are you using to keep yourself from rejection, control your world, or attract attention?

3. What mistakes, sins, poor choices, or addictions need to be surrendered to Jesus today?

PRAYER

Search me, O God, and know my heart! Try me and know my thoughts! And see if there be any grievous way in me, and lead me in the way everlasting! (Psalm 139:23–24)

—CHAPTER SIX—
A LOOK BACK, A STEP FORWARD

The ideal man bears the accidents of life with dignity and grace, making the best of circumstances.—Aristotle

GLEAMING FROM REFLECTION

There are no perfect parents or perfect children, only those pretending to be. During young adulthood, the twenties and thirties, when one moves out of their family home and establishes an independent life is when a person begins to gain perspective on family patterns that may be tripping them. This physical removal from the dynamics of one's family of origin begins the process of individuation by providing the time and space to evaluate oneself separate from the current family system. In the best-case scenario, the parents of the adult child lovingly encourage this separation, culminating years of building individuality, independence, and healthy boundaries, helping usher in the needed space without clinging too heavily to their adult child. Only then can the process of gathering, processing, and discarding take place as the newfound adult finds their own place in the world.

Memories of my (Jean's) family of origin are clouded by my parents' turbulent marriage and my mom's explosive temper. I became super vigilant, constantly on guard to foresee or forestall impending triggers that could shatter the peace. When I was in the third grade, I would hide the latest *Ladies Home Journal* magazine in my room to read the monthly article, "Can this Marriage Be Saved?" Later in my career, while conducting parental seminars, I would jokingly comment I have been doing marital therapy since the third grade. As a result, I became very good at discerning and empathetically responding to the needs of others but was not good at acknowledging my own feelings or meeting my own needs.

PATTERNS FROM THE PAST

All of us have painful memories, to a greater or lesser degree, from our childhood. Again, we choose between remaining stuck by continually recycling the past or resolving the past by facing it honestly and using it as a launching pad to the future. God has a plan for each person's life. When we let go of the past, we are ready to be molded by God for his future use. "'For I know the plans I have for you,' declares the Lord, 'plans for welfare and not for evil, to give you a future and a hope'" (Jeremiah 29:11).

Family patterns from the past affect our present relationships without us necessarily being aware of it. Some are beneficial, some are not. The pain generated from these imperfect interactions with our parents or siblings frequently go unaddressed. A façade is often drawn to mask our incompleteness and portray everything as perfect, or a wall is constructed to ease the pain and insulate us from feelings. As adults, it is necessary to look back to examine what is behind our walls and façades. Have we adopted behavioral patterns which prevent us from being close to others? Is lack of confidence preventing us from developing our strengths and talents or achieving our goals?

We all carry around inside our heads an inner script regarding our self-worth. The marquee is composed of our thoughts and feelings concerning our love for ourselves. If positive, it reads, "I love being me, I can do it, I learn from my mistakes." If negative it reads, "I am only loveable if … I'm ashamed to be me, I'm inadequate, I'm hopeless." Self-worth, the core of inner strength, involves unconditional acceptance of self, regardless of one's faults. Although people with strong self-worth want to achieve, they can handle failure—it doesn't defeat them. The ability to accept and feel good about oneself is an indication of positive self-worth. Ultimately, knowing yourself is realizing whom God created you to be and having the vulnerability to live that truth.

CHOOSE THE TRUTH

The first step in the pursuit of truth is choosing the truth about you. The plumb line for truth is God's Word. Play a new script if an old script plays tunes in your head that you are unlovable, inadequate, or will never be good enough to please anybody. Choose God's truth, which is you are beautiful, a masterpiece, created in God's image—unique and valuable (Genesis 1:27, Ephesians 2:10). Our primary identity is belonging to God's family. We are who we are in relation to others. Most importantly, we draw our identity from our impact on others. We all long to make a difference, find significance, to know we belong, to be loved. God is the source of true love. Jesus died for you and sent the Holy Spirit to help you. One can't feel whole without knowing and feeling the love of God. One can't feel whole without intentional acceptance of this truth. One can only feel and be loved in relationships first with God, then others.

Our self-worth and our view of God are usually a reflection of our parents' attitudes toward us as children. The extents that we felt cherished and affirmed by our parents provide our models for measuring our default amount of self-worth. If our parents' attitudes toward us were characterized by neglect, criticism, and rejection, then our self-worth is likely diminished, leaving some feeling we are unworthy of being loved. Others may feel they need to earn their parents' approval through performance. In this case, one's view of God will falsely follow the internal script that says it's necessary to earn God's love through good deeds rather than acknowledging God's grace and acceptance is a gift.

Thus, looking inside is necessary, however painful it may be. Finding your authentic self is rooted in truth and reality, not denial or illusion.

TIES THAT BIND TOO TIGHTLY

The familiar refrain, "I give this daughter in marriage ..." may all too often be empty words. In many instances, parents do not give their children in marriage, but rather accompany them into the marriage, preserving the psychological umbilical cord between the parent and child. Although marriage is for adults, often only the child from the past, existing inside many adults, repeats the marriage vows. Thus, an assortment of parents and in-laws are in the marital bed, calling the shots, and stomping out the seeds of intimacy. While many cry at weddings, overcome by the beauty of the moment or with joy, I (Jean) always cry at weddings realizing the rose-colored glasses are coming off and 20/20 vision is being restored. The road ahead will be difficult.

A friend in her sixties, reminiscing, said, "I wanted to go to a teacher's college. My father thought I should go to Katie Gibbs, a secretarial school, so I could find a job in business and marry a businessman. I went to Gibbs but dropped out after one semester because I hated accounting." Later, she married a businessman who was quite wealthy for a time.

He tried to take care of her and made her decisions for her—just like her father.

Family therapists refer to families such as these, where boundaries between members are blurred, as "enmeshed." Members are overly involved with each other. In enmeshed families, there is a heightened sense of belonging, in many cases with family members denying reality to present themselves as perfect. Individual exploration and problem solving are discouraged, resulting in lost autonomy. Within family circles, a small repertoire of behaviors is considered correct. This myopic focus distorts vision and family truths often conflict with realities in the broader world.

Instead of expanding one's reality and knowledge base to a broader perspective, thereby acquiring individual values and etching out one's own meaning and purpose in life, members of enmeshed families are stuck together like glue forsaking growth and change. They experience "letting go anxiety." Yet only as an individual "lets go" and begins to separate psychologically from their family of origin can the individual gain enough distance to perceive family relationships in a more realistic light and discover who they are. Until that time, the person is not available to form an intimate relationship with another.

If family ties are too binding, members only feel comfortable and complete within their own family circle. The need to feel close or belong, translated as loved, overshadows the need to experience one's own self and forge a unique identity.

All too often, we carry these fused parent/child relations from our family of origin into our family of choice. The relationship between our children and ourselves becomes too intense. Clear lines between the concerns, responsibilities, and privileges of parents versus children are not established, thus blurring the boundary between the parent's and child's selves. Often the child becomes involved in issues or receives privileges that should belong to the parents. Instead of working on their own issues, the child becomes entangled with the parents' issues. The growth of autonomy is thwarted.

Sam and LLF

This brings to mind two very different scenarios in cases referred to me. The first concerns a lack of motivation. The second concerns a lack of independence. In both cases, the boundaries between mother and son are blurred. Both boys sacrificed developing their own interests and strengths for over-involvement in their mother's life.

Sam, an only child of divorced parents, was a bright six-year-old in the first grade, who did not complete assignments. Both parents had drug addictions. In response to an inquiry about how things were going, he lamented, "Awful! The car won't start, we don't have money to pay the rent, and my mother forgot to take the pill!"

No wonder Sammy couldn't finish anything. He carried to school a bag of worries that belonged to his mother, when all he needed was a bag of lunch. Burdened by the worries in his mother's life, he had no room for learning.

Enjoying quite different circumstances was a cute curly-headed fourth grader who I mentally dubbed as Little Lord Fauntleroy (LLF). Although his teacher found him charming and sociable, LLF cleverly avoided work while at school. He much preferred to pile all his books into his backpack and lug them home, always returning the next day with all his work completed.

LLF was an only child with a doting mother and a hard-working business executive father. Their marriage was distant, and LLF was king of the household. His mother drew his bath, gave him back rubs, and served his breakfast in bed (ironically, these actions would have gone a long way to melt the ice in the marriage). Despite his father's protests, LLF not only used his father's expensive tools but left them out in the rain.

Considering the sense of entitlement generated by his mother's indulgence and interference, it made sense for LLF to bring his schoolwork home. Befitting his exalted family position, he had his own executive secretary tying up all the loose ends and completing unfinished tasks. Who needs to worry about mundane things like schoolwork? Thus, unknowingly and with good intentions, his mother reinforced his disobedience to two vital authority figures—his father and his teacher.

Although the family circumstances of Sam and LLF were different, the psychological dynamics were similar. Both mothers were overly close to their sons and had difficulties affirming their child's emerging self. Both boys experienced a heightened sense of togetherness with their mothers diverting them from exploring their own interests and needs. Neither father had a healthy relationship with his son. In both cases, the sons were treading into places their fathers had belonged. Boundaries were blurred.

If this pattern is not interrupted, youngsters will give up efforts to develop their own identity, which is essential for positive self-worth. Instead, the children develop a false self, based upon parental approval. Their thoughts and feelings are filtered through the perceptions of others, robbing them of a sense of their own self-being. They depend upon others to make their decisions and to provide them with a sense of internal security and worthwhileness. People-pleasing becomes their addiction.

TIES THAT INSULATE AND ISOLATE

On the other end of the spectrum are families where the boundaries between individuals are rigid—more like walls. Relationships are distant. Communication is on the intellectual or practical level. Feelings and dreams are rarely discussed. Because feelings are seldom shared, "I love you" is seldom heard. Independence and autonomy flourish, but intimacy and emotionality are rare. Members go their separate ways and are not comfortable together. Family members derive their sense of worth from their accomplishments. Productivity is the addiction rather than people.

Family therapists refer to these configurations of behaviors as a disengaged family. Whereas members of enmeshed families have "letting go anxiety," members of disengaged families have "getting close anxiety." A skewed sense of independence makes it difficult for individuals to receive love and support from others.

When I think of disengaged families, a scene from the movie *Annie Hall*[1] comes to mind. Annie, a Protestant from the Midwest, brings her New York Jewish friend, played by Woody Allen, home for Easter dinner to meet her parents.

The family is seated at the dinner table most properly with ample space between each member. Conversation is about a neighbor who just bought a new tractor. The real issue of Annie's love affair with a Jew is never discussed.

In sharp contrast, Woody is thinking about his family at the Passover table, crowded together, eating each other's food, finishing each other's sentences, discussing in detail their latest health problems. Why the attraction? His style, learned in a family that is intrusive and excessively involved with one another, feels like warmth to Annie coming from cold cognitive beginnings. Her strong sense of individuality was like a breath of fresh air to Woody, who was suffocated by togetherness. Rather than going through the long painful process of becoming a whole person, opposites attract in the ill-found hope that two such halves make a whole. They don't.

For a person from a disengaged family to form an intimate relationship, the walls will have to come down one brick at a time. The person will need to stop thinking and start feeling. Intimacy requires getting in touch with the array of tender feelings. For some, the thawing out process may require lifting any repression and isolation to get in touch with the pain required for healing and rebuilding.

Balancing Togetherness and Autonomy

Families at their best learn to balance togetherness and autonomy. Marriages at their best work constructively and enable such balance, with togetherness complementing respect for differences and individualization.

The desired outcome of marriage is to fulfill two goals. The first is making us feel loved and valued for the person we currently are. The second is to encourage growth. A balance is maintained between the need to feel loved and to experience one's own identity. The differences, instead of sameness, between family members are cherished and cultivated. This first requires awareness of each member.

The wise woman recognizes both husband and wife need to feel loved and need to identify and develop their unique God-given purpose. When both husband and wife place Jesus as the head of their marriage they become closer to God and each other. Encouraging and tapping into each other's strengths and talents makes their union more fulfilling.

William S. Paley, founder of the CBS network, was fond of relating his father's reaction to his desire to enter the radio business. Although his father offered him a position in the family cigar business, he encouraged his son to follow the dream that beckoned him to radio. The father told his son, "If you fail you will come to the cigar business with more enthusiasm. If you succeed, you will lead a much richer life."[2]

DIFFERENTIATION

It is important to be able to affirm your distinct goals separate from those around you. The ability to do this while remaining close to the important people in your life determines your level of differentiation, according to Murray Bowen. A person claims their own beliefs and convictions separate from others through critical thinking rather than feeling-driven "I" statements: "this is what/who I am," and "what I will/will not do." New knowledge or experience gleaned from growth drives the differentiated self to change from within. Confidence grows with understanding one's self and knowing who they are separate from others.

Less differentiated people are dominated by their feelings—feelings dominate over objective reasoning most of the time. They do not distinguish feelings from facts, and base major life decisions on what feels right. Primary life goals are oriented around love, happiness, comfort, and security. Life energy goes into seeking love and approval or attacking the significant other for not providing it. There is little energy left for goal-directed activity.

In contrast, more differentiated people have an increased capacity to distinguish between feelings and objective reality. They are operationally clear about the difference between feeling and thinking, and routinely make decisions based on critical thought, not personal feelings.

The more differentiated each partner is, the greater the likelihood for a happy union. Healthy families have clear boundaries between each member and each subsystem. Members accept responsibility for their own actions and feelings.

Being your truest self and differentiation are similar but not the same. The key difference is the truest self recognizes and relies on a relationship with God or at the very least, a higher power. In contrast, differentiation emphasizes the experiences and knowledge of the individual.

Over the years, I increasingly surrendered my life to Jesus, lessening my focus on the principles of psychology. I realized Jesus is the only healer. Without Jesus as Lord and Savior, the false self is in control, even for a well-differentiated self—a rather scary prospect we see in the world today.

This largely goes back to epistemology and the basis that Christianity is the only faith requiring admittance of a need for a grace-filled Savior. Without this directive of objective morality providing a compass to understand what is acceptable, life is like a boat without oars or anchor, subject to the waves and winds as the storms of life ebb and flow. Feelings come, go and change. Instead, with Jesus as director and healer, life is securely anchored, and we are able to follow God's guidance as a loving father, while also differentiating ourselves from others and the surrounding world. We understand where we end and where others begin. We understand the dignity, beauty, freedom, and preciousness that is our one life, extending that same understanding of real love to others. We take care of ourselves and others by knowing this dignity rooted in Christ, as God's precious creation.

This understanding beckons us out of stormy waters, out of the mire of past dysfunctions. We are led to try again for something healthy, lasting, and meaningful. God gives us the resolve to look back at our journey and use the dirt of the past as rich soil to nourish future wildflowers. Knowledge becomes seeds scattered in dark unseen places, in what would otherwise look like mud, and we patiently wait for hope to spring forth.

PRACTICES TO PONDER

1. What did you learn from your parents about handling conflict? Consider behaviors such as listening, compromising, yelling, blaming, crying, sarcasm, and avoidance.

2. Ask yourself: Am I better at giving or receiving love?

3. What patterns learned in my family of origin need to be changed?

PRAYER

Do not be conformed to this world, but be transformed by the renewal of your mind, that by testing you may discern what is the will of God, what is good and acceptable and perfect. (Romans 12:2)

—CHAPTER SEVEN—
SOWING AND REAPING

WISDOM IS OPEN TO REASON.

As you reflect on what you just read regarding family systems and healthy family functioning, you may need to stop and ponder your own family of origin. Take time and space to reflect on the good and bad, checking yourself for knee-jerk reactions to your spouse or kids. It is easy to continue patterns experienced growing up either because you think it worked, or because you're at odds with what you experienced. Either way, this is not the best, most mindful way to relate to others, or to parent your kids.

This was the case with Aiden's dad.

Aiden, a large, gawky first grader, got into fight after fight with classmates at school and his dad did nothing about it. I learned that Mom was the disciplinarian and Dad disagreed with most every attempt she made to correct Aiden. Dad had grown up with an abusive alcoholic mom who disciplined him with spankings that turned into beatings. As a result, discipline to Dad meant something horrible and painful. His mother never established clear rules and expectations, with choices and consequences that would teach him how to achieve those on his own. Instead, she berated him, calling even innocent and expected behavior "wrong." He was broken, having never felt understood, heard, or helped as a boy. His sense of shame grew with every beating. Now, as a dad, he was determined never to correct or punish (and therefore hurt) his son.

The result: Aiden had no self-control or respect for his parents, himself, or anyone else, and got away with everything. Mom was frustrated because every time she tried to correct and help Aiden, Dad shot down her authority. Dad could see Aiden created and faced growing problems but felt clueless about what to do and contributed to the bad behavior by allowing it.

Aiden's dad needed help to rethink discipline—where it was good, and how it could go awry. He needed to realize his experiences as a boy were of abuse, and recognize their difference to discipline, which means "to teach." He needed assurance that true love for a child involves correcting and teaching him, not coercing or abdicating guidance altogether.

How could he change his attitudes about discipline to better parent his son? How could he learn to work together with his wife to be a united front for Aiden?

Thinking intentionally and reflectively is a start. No matter your family background, you learned patterns. Digging into those roots will help you grow into being the best spouse, and parent, you can be—the one God wants, who sows wisdom into family relationships. The one who, with the help of God and the guidance of the Holy Spirit, changes and breaks patterns of behaviors that may run many generations deep. The wise woman realizes she can redirect her family's historical patterns of behavior in a way that future generations will look upon and, though flawed, call good, and she takes this opportunity. She moves toward love instead of running from fear as she pioneers a new way, separate from what she knew before. The Holy Spirit fuels her breath and thought, God directs, and Jesus is her brother and friend that goes alongside—comforting and redirecting.

LEARNING FROM REFLECTION

Begin by writing down some of the most formative incidents from your childhood. What happened? How did you feel? What did you do? How did your parents react? How did it change you?

There is power in writing. Acknowledge what happened and begin to peel back the layers of your experiences like an onion, understanding your own reactions.

First consider an outer layer—the outcomes, your experiences. What were helpful, corrective, instructive, or guiding forces for you? Why? Make a list of these positives and any negatives, like what felt hurtful, harmful, spirit-crushing, frustrating, and why.

Now examine the interior layer—identify your emotional vulnerabilities and strengths. For example, maybe a parent's harsh and authoritarian discipline has left you like Aiden's dad, struggling to trust or forgive, full of so much shame you fear failing and even succeeding. Or maybe your strengths are you're quick to correct things, you follow through, you don't repeat mistakes, and you're consistent.

Consider how each quality influences your responses to your children or spouse. You'll quickly see how you can attach what you've felt as a child to how you react now. Once you know where you want to be more mindful, you can begin to take powerful steps forward that will help you with your spouse and kids. Knowing is the first step toward change and becoming who God designed you to be.

DIGGING UP JEAN'S ROOTS

In my family of origin, the goal was to be competent, responsible, and productive. God was not in the picture, so our god became money. Work was the addiction. Roles were clearly defined by gender. My older brother was Mr. Outside, cutting the lawn or shoveling the snow. I was my mom's helper and confidante, her right hand in the kitchen, becoming confident and competent in cooking and household tasks in elementary school.

When, during World War II, Caroline, our full-time maid, quit to work in a defense plant, I assumed many of her household and food preparation duties. My brother and I dutifully did what was expected of us while my sister, who was six years younger, rebelled, doing no chores.

While preparing food together, my mother would enthrall me with stories about her childhood. Born in 1908 and raised in a large Catholic family, my mom was the youngest of eight siblings. My sense of God and emerging faith was nurtured through stories about my grandmother, who died before I was born, and her siblings. Her oldest brother, Anthony, stricken with tuberculosis, had been sent home to die following treatment at a sanatorium. Conducting a prayer vigil, my grandmother and her sisters knelt beside his deathbed day and night, praying for him to be healed. During the second week, there were subtle signs of improvement. They continued to pray and soon Tony was healed.

My parents were both the youngest in large families where hard work and responsibility were valued while love and nurturing were scarce. Although I am sure my parents loved each other, their marriage was extremely conflictual. Often at night I would hear them arguing, hurling angry insults at each other, the fury sometimes erupting into physical attacks. I hid under my blankets in an effort to disappear, to calm my fear and anxiety. Exposure to this anger gave me a fear of discord and no experience with healthy conflict resolution. I focused on maintaining or restoring peace at any cost. As a result, I became good at reading other people's emotions while denying my own. In my thirties, I deliberately began working on healthy expression of anger.

My mom was one of the first women's libbers. I loved hearing her stories about when she was twelve years old collecting rent for her father who was in the building and real estate business. In her raccoon coat (this was during World War I), she drove his Model-T Ford feeling so important. Birth control was one issue she focused on. According to my mother, who observed the plight of her four older sisters during the depression who had too many children, grew fat, and lost their houses—birth control was the solution. Later, when a priest would not allow her to receive communion due to her practice of birth control, she gave up her religion and, with it her faith, feeling hurt and resentful. Throughout my mom's life she suffered from depression, heightened anxiety, and rage attacks. She had a lot of strength, but not a lot of self-worth. Survival, not self-esteem, was the fashion of the time.

Love was delivered in actions rather than words. My dad had a caring and giving spirit. As a teenager, I remarked our recreation room would be enhanced if we had a jukebox. A week later, my dad arrived with a jukebox, making me feel like the coolest kid on the block. As we grew older, my dad was quick to finance a dream or pay for a fender bender. I too enjoy giving gifts and supporting purposes and passions, a trait I inherited from my father.

As an adult, I needed to uncover the dysfunctional, exhausting habits of people-pleasing and perfectionism. I needed to learn how to express my thoughts and feelings in a healthy manner. My mother, remembering her experiences collecting rent for her father, longed to have a career in real estate. Of German ethnicity, my father felt a woman's place was in the home and, as a businessman and good provider, considered my mother's ambitions an insult to him, thus thwarting her every attempt to reach her goal. I needed to learn to push against the restrictive views of my father and forge my own identity and career path. Only gradually, as my career emerged, did my father begin to realize the benefits of women having a purpose beyond childrearing and household management.

DIGGING UP JESSICA'S ROOTS

My parents have always been hardworking and resilient people who have had to overcome numerous traumas in their own early lives. As an infant, my father's dad walked out of his life, leaving a gaping hole where a father should have been. His mother battled lifelong mental illness. My mom also would grow up without a father figure, having lost her father, who died young in her early adolescence, among other key formative traumas. Thus, I was born into a legacy of unhealed trauma. I have great compassion toward my parents for what they faced early on and for the ways they strove to improve their situations and for bettering the lives of their children.

Growing up, I loved that my mom was always willing to support my DIY room redecoration efforts. I also loved watching her cook—the way she added ingredients by instinct and improvisation instead of by recipe. I love to cook that way today.

I also loved my dad's spontaneity. He was an expert fort-builder and day-adventure-seeker. We would get up in the morning on some weekends and drive from Big Bear, California, to the nearest outlet mall a couple of hours away. I had so much fun with my dad—grabbing a special something to eat and then browsing stores. I'd always come home with a new pair of shoes or some fun accessories.

Sometimes he'd decide to turn a day excursion with my brothers and me into a trip to Las Vegas or to Mexico for the weekend. On trips to San Felipe, Mexico, we bought hammocks from locals, slept under grass cabanas, and woke up surrounded by ocean air and seagulls.

Amidst such polaroid memories, however, exists the theme of trauma which colors the feeling of my memories. My younger years also consisted of a series of traumatic experiences and at times seasons of complete loss and instability. I now understand these seasons to be attributed, largely, to various forms of mental illness when the color of trauma became the unconscious filter through which I viewed the world early on. The color was dark and foreboding and lurked around the next corner.

In my childhood, there was no unpacking of feelings, no discussion of mental illness, though the generational links were long and the hurts deep. Instead, my feelings seemed to settle in my throat, the feeling of withholding tears. Ironically, or not, I often had recurring strep and other throat and body maladies as a child and into adulthood. Having begun to understand and heal, I now wonder the ways they are linked.

From birth to age ten, my family had moved nearly a dozen times within four different cities and two states. All these conditions made forging relationships and keeping friends very difficult. It was scary enough to invite friends into the chaos of my life without knowing at any moment if I would have to start the exhausting work of loss and unfamiliarity all over again. I became a shy little girl and felt I had no voice. I was paralyzed when it came to speaking to adults. I lived inside my head, and my body became conditioned to operating under a fight or flight state of being. Those early years are an important part of my story and need to be mentioned to give explanation to my necessary and still ongoing journey of healing.

My parents began taking us to church regularly when I was in middle school. I was baptized as a teenager, sealing the faith that was growing and would continue to grow in me as I learned more about Jesus. Looking back, I see how God was always working in my messy life. I am so thankful for the faith heritage passed down to me by my parents, from their parents, given from their parents. This legacy of faith is a rich gift and though I don't know a lot about my extended family tree, one thing is clear—Jesus was in it! My family tree has been a messy branch in the seasons and years extended from the tree of life.

When I entered college, I was able to begin to understand myself out of the context of my immediate family and upbringing. In looking back, I recognize that, at eighteen, I began the process of unlearning and re-conditioning myself in particular ways I needed to heal—especially in the areas of emotional regulation and boundary setting and in understanding the generational struggles I had inherited. I chose to attend a small Christian university because I knew I needed to understand God's Word and allow him to heal and direct me.

In hindsight, I recognize my actions were not always intentional, but in first seeking God, I came to understand myself more, which catapulted from that point on into my ongoing drive toward wholeness in Christ. I sought counseling in college with a couple of okay therapists and shopped for therapists for several years until I met one who really took the time to care about and understand my story and who was a source of profound healing.

This exemplifies why the work of a counselor is essential to healing for those of us whose upbringing didn't involve talking through and addressing problems and emotions in a healthy way. The problems and emotions don't simply go away. If avoided, as an adult we are left with childhood feelings that still surmount, efface, and manifest as in a neglected child yet now in an adult body. We remain children in grown bodies unless our emotions are processed with the same vigor, time, and commitment one would take to parent a small child. I know because I was one until about my mid-twenties.

I saw a therapist regularly for seven years of my adult life and feel it is one of the healthiest gifts we can give ourselves. Working with various therapists has allowed me to uproot the deep-seeded pain left untended inside and to understand the compulsion that drives me back to what was while desperately clambering toward wholeness. In therapy, I found the freedom to cry out my hurt, to give it a name, a voice, and meaning, to express it freely, and to see truth in utmost safety while receiving loving encouragement. In this way, I have been able to honor and continue to integrate all parts of my story.

My primary counselor, Tom, will always be like a guardian angel to me for providing a haven in which I could heal, and who gave me a healthy space, time, and a place to be heard. I was acknowledged at my most authentic and raw places without judgment. Tom was the hands and feet of Jesus to me, and in that space of counseling, I was inspired to become a better listener. I became a better caregiver to those who are hurting and healing thanks to his example of stability and kindness. Later along on my healing journey, Jen, a kindred spirit and counselor, held me accountable to pursue my passions and gifts as she encouraged me to further live and speak truth. From Jen, I continued to practice listening to myself and understanding that I didn't have to be what I was not. I didn't have to strive harder or achieve more. I could listen to that still soft voice inside, and let it lead me.

There is much left unsaid about my upbringing and ongoing healing journey. I share a sprinkling here to give voice to those who might feel alone or silenced because of a traumatic background. You are not alone. I am now at a place where I can appreciate and take pride in my story—hardships, trauma, and all—knowing that it has given me a certain depth of understanding and insight. This depth is needed in pursuing many of my greatest passions. My story is not over, and there are numerous painful areas I am still working through. Yet, I now have a profound strength in knowing I am held in the mighty shadow of God, who leads me. I feel I now have a greater expanse in which to live than I once did. I feel more comfortable in my humanity and more trusting of God's goodness and his plan for me through life's recurrent pains and problems.

In the thick of messy, real life, I continue to ask these questions of myself: "What can I handle? What can I not handle? What do I need in a relationship?" I continue to learn that boundary setting is about me and not about controlling other people's behavior. The path is not always linear, but often takes revising, with some stops, backups, and restarts. The path is also not fixed. We are all entitled to regroup and restart again. One of the key lessons I have learned in this self-work is that my adult life is entirely my responsibility and with that comes the responsibility to care for myself in every way. As such, I insist upon pursuing an integrated life, where all parts can work together and make sense and walk in the way of truth and peace. I don't have to hide or fear any part of my story because I have worked through and am working through the most painful pieces, which has given way to profound freedom and peace. This has freed up tremendous headspace and energy to pursue many long-held callings which only in my late thirties do

I have the ability and clarity to pursue.

DIGGING UP YOUR ROOTS

Find a time and place where you can be alone with Jesus. We all want to be the women God calls us to be—our true selves in Christ. Although we become a member of God's family when we accept Jesus, all we know about family living comes from our original family. Relax and pray, asking Jesus to recall thoughts and feelings as you reflect on your childhood family atmosphere. Try to use words such as affirming, supportive, complaining, competitive, cooperative, conflictual, critical, abusive, angry, tense, close, distant, fun-loving, sociable.

Next, ponder your mother, considering her strengths and weaknesses. What were the good traits she passed along to you? Alternatively, what baggage do you now carry that you need to give to Jesus to heal?

For example, when I (Jean) think of my mother, my first thought was the memory of the last time I saw her, following her last stroke. Her beautiful, loving smile followed me as I left her hospital room with tears in my eyes (which still flow as I recall the scene). I felt loved by my mom. I also thank her for expecting and teaching me to be competent and responsible. My mom had a violent temper too. It made me afraid of anger in my twenties, becoming a peace-at-any-cost kind of woman. Over time I realized this attitude was not effective and, through the aid of psych courses and counseling, I learned healthy expression of anger.

Recall your relationship with your father. Similarly, consider messages you received regarding marriage, gender roles, parenting, family, money, sex, conflict, relationships, success. Looking at the past illuminates the future—always painful, but worth the price.

PRACTICES TO PONDER

1. What losses and pains in your life are waiting to be acknowledged and grieved?

2. What abilities, talents, and interests are lying dormant waiting to be cultivated?

3. Are you harboring a grudge that needs to be forgiven?

PRAYER

And it is my prayer that your love may abound more and more, with knowledge and all discernment, so that you may approve what is excellent, and so be pure and blameless for the day of Christ. (Philippians 1:9–10)

Lord Jesus, set me free to be the person you created me to be. Although I resist looking at the past and feeling the pain, I seek your guidance and direction. Help me learn what it means to examine the past and face honestly the patterns of behavior that need to be changed. I lift the pain to you, trusting that you will use it as a means of growth.

—CHAPTER EIGHT—
WISDOM AND THE AUTHENTIC SELF

I hope you live a life you're proud of. If you find that
you're not, I hope you have the strength to start all over
again.—*The Curious Case of Benjamin Button*[1]

DEFINING AUTHENTICITY

This is what I (Jess) know about what it means to live
authentically so far. In authenticity, we live comfortably
in ourselves—our hearts, minds, and actions align. We
become fierce editors of our lives, quickly deciphering,
"This is me. This is not me." Actions, words, and deeds
follow suit with the deep, God-given longings of our souls.
Truth is valued—not feared—however painful, because it
does not threaten, but helps us become more authentic.

This process requires taking the time to understand all
the parts and stages of who we have been, acknowledging
how our choices and experiences have affected us, in order
to arrive at the person we are today. We are continually
transforming. Hold hands with your five-year-old self
during the times that most frightened her, pat her hair, and
whisper, "It's going to be okay." Accept your humanity and
frailty while acknowledging the wonder of the life you've
been given. Take hold, with confidence, purpose, and hope,

your ability to live out the purpose for which God has called us and destined us before our birth.

Living in this mindset, there's no need to change or control others. We're free to see and love others in their authenticity. There's an understanding of where one person ends and another begins.

THE SOURCE OF AUTHENTICITY

Authenticity extends beyond the self. It must be rooted in one's creator. Jesus drew his identity, strength, and direction from the Father, daily seeking guidance and redirection. The end of his human life left behind the gift of the Holy Spirit. For Jesus, authenticity and connection with the Father meant not freedom from pain, but purpose from pain in human life for eternal significance.

Dr. Dan Allender in his book *Bold Love* reminds us, "To the degree that this life holds the possibility of 'getting something,' we will labor and flounder to achieve what only heaven can offer. On the other hand, to the degree that this life is viewed as a place of pilgrimage—a place where it is never honorable or right to build a lasting foundation—I am released to live and love through seeing my life used to advance your progress and joy in Christ."[2]

He goes on to say:

> We are to live with the ongoing cycle of anticipation/ sorrow. If we "admit" our deep desire is not fully met, then we can embrace the reality of the sojourner who has not yet found rest and peace. It is not "abnormal" to be empty, sad, and lonely at the deepest place in our souls that was fashioned for eternity—to be dissatisfied with the empty provisions of this world, sad over the destruction of beauty, lonely for the companionship of lost friendships. It is not only abnormal, but wrong to be otherwise.

The Wise Woman Within, becoming ever more authentic, knows this. She understands this was not the way life was supposed to be, and this is not the end of the story.

We try to forget, pretending we can make this life heaven on our way to heaven. We get it wrong even in the "best" of Christian circles with a strong basis in theology. Really understanding and mourning the realization that heaven will not be achieved here—that we are dying people who live in a dying world—frees us for the joy of understanding the seasons of this life. We are allowed to bloom within the experience of pain, realizing the holiness and joy despite and in the midst of pain. We don't flee from pain, at least not compulsively or in fear, but understandingly embrace all that happens with a lighthouse-like resilience in Christ. Therefore, we are not unfeeling mortar pillars, but warm-bodied, feeling believers who look at life straight on, inviting it to crash: hearing, seeing, and feeling the strength of the waves—invigorated by its splash and splendor.

FOR ALL

There is no system that binds the authentic self, or socioeconomic situation, if the authentic self is constantly in community with the heavenly Father. Take, for instance, the example of Jean and me (Jess). I was born in a trailer park in the eighties, in the armpit that is the California high desert. Jean, on the other hand, was born into an upper middle class midwestern family in the thirties. The worlds we entered were drastically different. The decades between us separate respective childhood experiences witnessing the bombing of Pearl Harbor during World War II from the fall of the Berlin Wall and the 9/11 terrorist attack. Yet our journeys of finding our authentic selves have been essentially the same—upward trajectories in line with our respective growth in Christ, our journeys of soul-growth and soul-work.

We rest in the scriptural truth that says, "And I am sure of this, that he who began a good work in you will bring it to completion at the day of Jesus Christ" (Philippians 1:6). Nobody, regardless of her background, culture, or record, is excluded from this process of good work. The process is offered to all of us. If the purpose of this life on earth is not earthly gain, then humanity's greatest authenticity is found in what is true always—communion with the creator, residing with God and others in mutual love and understanding, for always. This was and is God's intention—to reside with and enjoy his creation.

GROWTH

I know I am growing when I have a healthy indifference to the things of this world, craving more of God's Word and simply desiring his presence. External pressure has less hold, however much I may feel in my humanity, because I am more in tune with the Holy Spirit, as well as my eternal spirit, the one that will live forever.

We need this strength to love ourselves through tragedy and to relate to others in a genuine and loving way. Some of my most challenging and self-defeated days have come in marriage and parenting. These are countered by days which are so beautiful and wonderful—the ephemerality of it all causes pain of a good kind. Knowledge of life's brevity holds me accountable, allowing me to live in the moment. This is as real as life gets. For this brief time, we are called to love our spouses and children—we can't lose sight of that. The richest love this side of heaven is knowing one's authentic self-made whole in Jesus and offering that self to those God has called us to love. Only in first knowing this love for ourselves can we help our children and others to decipher it in themselves.

THE PROCESS AND PRACTICE

For me, this practice of authenticity and the desire to become wise in the Lord is not a finite task but is ongoing. I continually work out this practice within myself, and in the confidence of my husband and a few close friends. We never graduate from the practice of wholeness in Christ.

St. Benedict wisely stated, "Always we begin again."[3] Authenticity is a process of continual starts and stops—this fits, this doesn't, this is aligned with God's Word, this is not. Authenticity is recognizing the gray areas in my life where the way is unclear and asking for help when needed (Scripture, a counselor, a wise friend of integrity).

Authenticity also means embracing awkwardness and vulnerability while venturing to the unknown parts of myself to discover those parts that have been buried and hidden. Every door and every window inside the heart is opened, one by one.

Authenticity is continually seeking to grow, heal, and recover. My own journey has been costly and time consuming. As a result, chasms have formed between myself and others, where the living Word of truth flows between us and causes a natural separation. At the same time, the most meaningful relationships of my life have had space to flourish. I've had to learn to let myself be known and to know others in a more real way. This has been birthed out of understanding my worth and the dignity of all people in a new way. I have come to know myself intimately, which can be scary at times, faced with my greatest strengths and my many weaknesses. I've become acutely aware that seeing the worst in others is the condition of my own heart without God's moment-by-moment direction.

However, this growth has not come without having first been leveled. Often demolition is involved—a period of waiting and hoping for the future, a period that can feel like fear and anxiety of the unknown, as growth and change tends to feel. Often, it's in these broken places that God moves. God has changed my heart, so I now see my own brokenness in the brokenness of others. He has allowed me to see the good in others right next to the brokenness, just as he has allowed me to see the ways he uses my life for good amidst my own brokenness.

There continue to be lots of high highs and low lows. Over time, however, I've gained a peaceful stillness—a stillness that sometimes feels like the true me walking hand-in-hand in the warm grasp of Jesus, always there to comfort me. This peace ushers me forward and gives me confidence to continue my journey. God provides constancy and support through the ever-changing seasons and teaches us to love better through them if we have ears to hear and hearts willing to bloom perennially after life's many small deaths.

What It's Not

The search for one's authentic self is not an obsession with self, but rather caring about self and others enough to live and play in the way God has made us unique. Avoiding such careful introspection and interdependence is also costly, tangling others in the wake of our untended messes. There is so much strength in knowing we have the permission to live in this freedom as God has created us. The world is our backyard, and it needs our unique offering and gifts. We owe it to ourselves and others to carve out our true selves from the rubble so we may offer diamonds.

Finding My Authentic Self

In 2013, I found myself broken inside and knew I wasn't living authentically me. My job sucked the life out of me. My mental health was terrible. I drank too much wine nearly every night, and my thoughts and words were in a very dark place. Once I screamed so loud at my husband in the car that my voice went hoarse. I was face to face with someone I didn't want to be—an ugly version of myself. There was a volcanic cry deep within my soul that billowed forth with any stirring of fault lines just under the surface.

I made some challenging and trying decisions that year, which ultimately led to major growth and joy in my life. The process, which began before that year of working through some dysfunctions of my upbringing and my own issues, peaked under the pressures of marriage, a difficult job which consumed me in an unhealthy way, and infertility.

I quit my job and joked with a friend I would be taking a sixty-thousand-dollar nap now that I would be unemployed (which lasted all of two weeks). I prayed for miracles for my temper and marriage. I prayed I would see the faces of my children. I sought counselors and had several phone consultations before arriving in the office of a counselor to whom I drove fifty minutes each way to see nearly every week, once a week, for two years.

I felt crappy about myself in that season. In fact, Tom, my counselor at the time, asked me a simple question during that time. He asked me, "Do you like yourself?" Instead of answering, I started hysterically crying. I didn't like myself anymore. Yet that was my moment of transformation, when I was awake to the knowledge of my own misery, and it was there in my brokenness that I let go and welcomed God's leading. I knew how detached I felt from myself, which felt hopeless and terrible, but I also relied on the hope of God's plan for my life, which carried me through. I remembered the countless men and women of the Bible who walked with the Lord and trusted in him and yet lived in that space of suffering, whether self-made or inflicted upon them, or both. I began to understand that true faith often involves self-surrender. I also learned that suffering and hope often travel together with faith.

In the midst of my pain in that long season of suffering, there was a small voice deep inside that I didn't create myself, which whispered I was worth it, my husband was worth it, my marriage was worth it. This life is beyond myself, beyond my understanding, beyond my control. These inklings of faith ushered me forward. I had to rely on the Holy Spirit instead of my own flesh. My life transformed from this point forward.

Everything changed. How freeing to give up the self and trust in the Lord! This was the beginning of wisdom's rebuke and invitation to me in my adult life. As Proverbs 1:20–22 says, "Wisdom cries aloud in the street, in the markets she raises her voice; at the head of the noisy streets she cries out; at the entrance of the city gates she speaks: 'How long, O simple ones, will you love being simple? How long will scoffers delight in their scoffing and fools hate knowledge?'" I didn't know to name it as such then, but my moment of leveling was the soil of my life being tilled in a dramatic, holy way. I was now willing to listen, as the mattock of God's hand began breaking me up. Every weed had to go so seeds could be planted.

I got stronger each week, growing closer to that person I knew I could be inside—tugged along by a wiser version of me walking ahead, offering her hand.

Now I nearly cry when I look into the faces of my miraculous and gorgeous children. As I write this, my three-month-old son, Rocky, looks up at me and coos with the sweetest smile. In this moment, I see the purpose in the toil and process, more fully understanding the process of refinement, one God will continue to work out in me as my children grow. Every day, I answer the invitation to start over again—to give up the old ways in pursuit of a better, higher way.

PRACTICES TO PONDER

1. Is this the time to take an in-depth look at your life?
2. Those who seek Christian counseling often gain valuable insight and perspective.
3. Is spending time with God and his Son a top priority?

PRAYER

Jesus himself is the truth that set us free. He is the source of truth and the perfect standard of what is right. Not only does Jesus set us free from the consequences of sin, but also from our own deception. Jesus does not give us freedom to do what we want, but freedom to follow God.

Jesus's truth.

"For with you is the fountain of life; in your light do we see light." (Psalm 36:9)

—CHAPTER NINE—
KNOWING YOURSELF

> If you turn at my reproof, behold, I will pour out my
> spirit to you; I will make my words known to you.
> (Proverbs 1:23 NLT)

The source of love and the basis of our worth is our identity
in Christ. Without appreciating our own worth, we cannot
become the unique individuals God created us to be. "So God
created man in his own image, in the image of God he created
him; male and female he created them" (Genesis 1:27).

You can only know who you are when you know who
God is. Knowing God and knowing ourselves are intricately
related. In 1536, John Calvin wrote, "Our wisdom ... consists
almost entirely of two parts: the knowledge of God and of
ourselves. But as these are connected together by many
ties, it is not easy to determine which of the two precedes
and gives birth to the other."[1]

God tells us from the beginning of the Bible that we were
made on purpose, for a purpose. I (Jean) have paraphrased
and personalized the following important Scripture
passages to share with you.

> You're my handiwork, my one-of-a-kind masterpiece,
> made to do good works I've planned long ago just for
> you (Ephesians 2:10–12).

Before I knit you together in your mother's womb, I knew you and set you apart to do something special (Jeremiah 1:5).

In grace, I've given you different gifts for doing certain things well, so if your gift is serving others serve well. If you're a teacher, then teach well. If your gift is encouraging others, be encouraging. If it's giving, then generously give. If you are an able leader, then take the responsibility seriously, and if you have a gift for showing kindness to others, do it gladly (1 Corinthians 12:27–31).

GUIDED

Jesus's love and obedience for the Father and the Father's love for his Son serve as a model for us. Jesus instructed, "As the Father has loved me, so have I loved you. Abide in my love. If you keep my commandments, you will abide in my love, just as I have kept my Father's commandments and abide in his love" (John 15:9–10). Here, God sets the pattern of true love, the basis of all relationships. When you love someone, you are willing to give freely to the point of self-sacrifice. God paid the highest price he could pay with the death of his Son. Jesus accepted our punishment, paid the price for our sins. Now, Jesus offers us the new life He bought for us.

In this the love of God was made manifest among us, that God sent his only Son into the world, so that we might live through him. In this is love, not that we have loved God but that he loved us and sent his Son to be the propitiation for our sins. Beloved, if God so loved us, we also ought to love one another. (1 John 4:9–11)

CHERISHED TIME WITH THE CREATOR

Singles, partnered, married—all of us who seek solitude with Jesus and live on a daily diet of his Word will become more Christ-like. As we continually feed on a diet of Scripture, the Word will work in us—uprooting sin, transforming our thoughts, and bringing us closer to God. Once we have accepted Jesus as Lord of our lives, our status changes from that of God's creation to God's sons and daughters. Just as it is important for children to spend relationship time with their earthly fathers, so it is with their heavenly Father. One way to nourish the life of God in our soul is by establishing a daily quiet time to be alone with him, praying and reading his Word.

In his book, *The Practice of Godliness*, Jerry Bridges writes, "We need a planned time each day for reading or studying the Bible. Every Christian who makes progress spends regular time in the Bible. There is simply no other way."[2]

> All Scripture is breathed out by God and profitable for teaching, for reproof, for correction, and for training in righteousness. (2 Timothy 3:16)

DATE WITH GOD

In 1979, while I attended Saint Paul's Episcopal Church in Darien, Connecticut, the pastor, Everett L. Fullum, cautioned the congregation about the days ahead. As the Scriptures were taught and acted upon, individuals might find themselves drawn closer to the living God and increasingly open to the Lord—growing and maturing. For some, the opposite might happen—constricting and tightening with the teaching, leaving as the atmosphere becomes intolerable. As predicted, over time, a few did leave. Many more, however, stayed and grew. I was one of them. "God has that effect on people. We cannot deal with his word very much without having it step on our toes. It points out things like a searchlight and demands a response. That can be dangerous ... to old ways of life," Father Fullum warned.

I began having a daily quiet time with God under the influence of Father Fulham's teaching. I am one of those people who can testify the words of the Gospel impact you. Not only did I gain intellectual understanding, but also most importantly, the words softened and transformed my heart. My life has never been the same after being transformed by God's Word. Thirty-nine years later, I walk hand-in-hand with God, experiencing his love and guidance.

> Oh how I love your law!
> It is my meditation all the day.
> Your commandment makes me wiser than my enemies,
> for it is ever with me.
> I have more understanding than all my teachers,
> for your testimonies are my meditation. (Psalm 1:1–3).

Oswald Chambers writes in the devotional, *My Utmost for His Highest*, "Prayer is the way that the life of God in us is nourished. Prayer is not about changing things externally, but one of working miracles in a person's inner nature."[3] Without faith anchored on the Bible, you have no rudder to guide you, no power of prayer and the Holy Spirit, no knowledge of God's choices for your life.

A Letter from Nelson Mandela

For twenty-seven years Nelson Mandela was a political prisoner in South Africa for his role as leader in the African National Congress in its struggle against the apartheid regime. His previously unpublished letters from prison remind us that Mandela used a horrific situation for good by using his prison cell as a place to meditate and cultivate a spiritual life.

> You may find that a metaphorical cell is an ideal place to learn to know yourself, to search realistically and regularly the process of your mind and feelings.

In judging our progress as individuals, we tend to concentrate on external factors such as one's social position, influence and popularity, wealth, and standard of education. These are, of course, important in measuring one's success in material matters and it is perfectly understandable if many people exert themselves to achieve all these. But considering internal factors may be even more crucial in assessing one's development as a human being. Honesty, sincerity, simplicity, humility, pure generosity, absence of vanity, readiness to serve others—qualities which are within easy reach of every soul—are the foundation of one's spiritual life.

Development in matters of this nature is inconceivable without serious introspection, without knowing yourself, your weaknesses, and your mistakes. If nothing else, the cell provides an opportunity to look daily into your conduct, overcoming the bad and developing the good. Regular meditation, say about fifteen minutes a day before you turn in, can be fruitful in this regard. It may be difficult at first to pinpoint the negative features in your life, but the tenth attempt may yield rich results. Never forget that a saint is a sinner who keeps on trying.[4]

> Oh, how I love your law!
> I meditate on it all day long.
> Your commands are always with me
> and make me wiser than my enemies.
> I have more insight than all my teachers,
> for I meditate on your statutes.
> (Psalm 119:97–99)

PRACTICES TO PONDER:
ESTABLISHING A DATE WITH GOD

1. Be deliberate—select a time early in the morning.

2. Find a quiet place to sit honestly before the Lord. The focus should be on God's presence. Notice the grace there available to you.

3. Bring your Bible and favorite devotionals.

4. Take a yummy beverage or snack to enjoy.

5. Focus on being in God's presence.

PRAYER

Jesus, allow us to see and know what is true today. Give us the courage to see our own part in what is wrong in our lives. Correct us when we are wrong and teach us, gently, what is right. We thank you for your overwhelming and unconditional love for us in this process and for leading us beside still waters and restoring our soul (Psalm 23:2). Amen.

—CHAPTER TEN—
TRANSFORMATION

Therefore, as you received Christ Jesus the Lord, so walk in him, rooted and built up in him and established in the faith, just as you were taught, abounding in thanksgiving. (Colossians 2:6–7)

THE SECOND TIME AROUND

GK was fond of recalling how we met—on Langdon Street abutting the University of Wisconsin, Madison campus during my freshman year. He longed to date me, but every time he saw me, I was on the arm of another man. Over a decade later when he heard I was getting a divorce, as he was, the pursuit began. His love and care were comforting after the heartbreak of my marriage. My heart warmed to see him having fun playing ball with my two young sons. Three years later, we were married on August 6, 1965.

I have a drawer full of love letters GK wrote to me. He was a gifted writer and wonderful at expressing himself, very charismatic. He helped me write my thoughts down at the end of the day when I was frustrated with my dyslexia, when my letters and words began jumbling together. He'd say, "Jean, you have such profound thoughts. You just speak and I'll write them down for you." In compiling my notes for this book, I can see him smiling from heaven encouraging me forward.

Infidelity

GK traveled extensively as a VP of sales for Gillette, Inc. At times, when he returned, I noticed lipstick on his shirt. He was red-green color-blind, so he couldn't distinguish the color. With time, I became increasingly aware of his preference for women and being close to women at work—more red flags alerted me of his unfaithfulness. I never had a jealous nature, and I am very social, but I gradually became more aware of his tendency to form very close relationships with women. Over time, I confronted him about his behaviors, looks between him and a gal that struck a thought, but he never admitted anything. Denial was his chief defense. Although I knew intellectually the earlier you address a problem the better the results, I let it ride, not ready for the emotional and financial impact on my and my sons' lives. I did not want this to disrupt my sons' educations or their future plans. GK and I were both living behind curtains of denial, just for very different reasons. Not confronting the truth or addressing sinful behavior will always cause continual damage, pain, and wounds to the heart.

During the ensuing years, we became "empty nesters" as both of my sons completed their university studies and were exploring new roles for the future. Death hung over us like a dark cloud, when suddenly my father died of a heart attack, and shortly thereafter, GK's mother took a turn for the worst, breathing her last breath, followed by GK's dad passing, all within one year. The combined loss of his parents as well as a business setback had a debilitating impact on GK. Reluctant to discuss the matter, he became irritable and distant. In hindsight, I can see now that I was busy and preoccupied having just begun doctoral studies and working full time.

BETRAYAL

When GK traveled, I became aware of discrepancies between where GK said he was and where he really was. I filed for divorce when my suspicion became a name. GK did not want a divorce. Anger and hurt filled me as details of his transgressions emerged. He destroyed my trust. During this extremely difficult time, I stopped trying, striving, denying, and enabling. One evening while sitting in the dark praying, I realized my anger and pain were eating me alive. I couldn't think or move on. I felt hopeless. "Jesus help me," I cried in anguish and despair. I invited God into the whole ugly mess of my life, and gave Jesus my broken heart to comfort.

The healing process began. I came to the end of myself and surrendered my life to Jesus when I realized the folly of self-sufficiency and the blasphemy of being god of my own life, feeling broken and empty because of failure and pain. In this prayer, I handed my broken heart to Jesus for healing, my mind for his thoughts, and my soul for his restoring.

SURRENDER AND REPENTANCE

Instantly, I was clothed in a warm glow. "Come to me" (Matthew 11:28). In so doing, the power of the Holy Spirit invaded my soul equipping me with the supernatural redemptive power of Jesus. The Wise Woman was born. Paul Tillich wrote that suffering invades the normal patterns of life and reminds you that you are not who you thought you were.[1] The depth of your soul is much deeper than you knew. Being broken open with this kind of pain and grief brings death to the ego. The self-centered voice of the ego must be quieted before a person can be capable of giving and receiving love. This only happens in the transforming power of the Holy Spirit.

I first felt the warm glow of Jesus's love. Awakened, as an intimate relationship with Jesus grew, I became painfully aware of my sinfulness. My self-sufficiency and denial trapped me in a world built on lies. My growing intimacy with Jesus awakened my need to live in the spirit and the truth. Following surrender, repentance was the first step to becoming closer to God.

CENTRALITY OF GOD

Respect and reverence of God is the beginning of wisdom. Our primary task is to give up our selfish self by placing Jesus at the center of our lives. For most of us, that means relinquishing control to Jesus. We are meant to focus our lives on God. As Jesus told us, "Love the Lord your God with all your heart and with all your soul and with all your mind. This is the great and first commandment. And a second is like it: You shall love your neighbor as yourself" (Matthew 22:37–39). Only in God do we find our true authentic identity.

If God is not the center of our lives, something else fills that space. Addictive behaviors often fill an empty longing where God belongs. I live in a gated golfing community, and golf becomes an obsession for many here. Golf is all many people in my neighborhood want to do and talk about—constantly practicing, taking lessons, buying new clubs, playing another eighteen holes. Golf becomes the center of their existence. Yet it is impossible to find peace and contentment with a game or even a person or career. Your ultimate belonging is with God. You can't complete yourself with anything else. "The fear of the Lord is the beginning of knowledge; fools despise wisdom and instruction" (Proverbs 1:7).

The WWW has faced the darkness within, and has come to the end of herself, seeking the healing light and love of Jesus. Our heavenly Father sent Jesus into this world to die on the cross and pay our sin debt. Only in this way can we be forgiven and receive a clean heart. To experience the presence of Jesus in your heart you need the empowering work of the Holy Spirit. As Paul writes, "For this reason I bow my knees before the Father, from whom every family in heaven and on earth is named, that according to the riches of his glory he may grant you to be strengthened with power through his Spirit in your inner being, so that Christ may dwell in your hearts through faith" (Ephesians 3:14-17).

The more room you make for Jesus in your heart the more you will be filled with his love. Spending time with Jesus is crucial to expanding the space in your heart—enjoy his presence, study the Word, and pray continually. God's goal is to make us holy like his son, Jesus—a long process that continues until we go to heaven. Gradually, as you put Jesus in the center of your life, you become less selfish and controlling, more peaceful and joyful. You notice relationships are harmonious and you enjoy more fruits of the spirit.

Changing how we think is an important part of a transformed life. Many faulty beliefs we hold are based on our surrounding culture or learned in our families of origin. These beliefs lead to us making decisions based on faulty criteria or assumptions. Decisions made on emotions can also lead us astray. When Jesus is the center of my life, my actions are aligned with Scripture, God's truth. Many of us have driven cars with the wheels not properly aligned, constantly pulling us in the wrong direction. In the same way, we get pulled off course when our goals do not align with those of Jesus for us.

The WWW has learned to listen to the gentle whisper of Jesus within her heart. "Give me understanding, that I may keep your law and observe it with my whole heart" (Psalm 119:34 NLT).

You are on the journey of becoming your truest self once you have come to the end of yourself, no longer controlling your own life by surrendering it all to Jesus. Think of it as an exciting journey to know and fulfill your designated purpose. God is at the center, guiding you on the path of utilizing your unique abilities, experiences, personality, and passions for his purpose. Walking with God, you are mindful of the Holy Spirit influencing your convictions, choices, and conduct. With gratitude in your heart, you will feel the joy and peace of his presence.

THE REBIRTHING PROCESS

Although I had already established a habit of daily prayer and Bible reading, following the divorce, I had an insatiable desire to spend more time in his Word and with his followers. God led me to a group of emotionally mature Christian women in my church. While praying, one of the leaders received a Bible passage, Hebrews 13:4–8, for me from God.

> Let marriage be held in honor among all, and let the marriage bed be undefiled, for God will judge the sexually immoral and adulterous. Keep your life free from love of money, and be content with what you have, for he has said, "I will never leave you nor forsake you." So we can confidently say, "The Lord is my helper; I will not fear; what can man do to me?" Remember your leaders, those who spoke to you the word of God. Consider the outcome of their way of life and imitate their faith. Jesus Christ is the same yesterday and today and forever.

At first, I was a bit miffed as I read these verses over and over. I had always honored my marriage vows. Now that I was divorced, God wanted me to continue to honor my marriage vows? Initially, I found these words harsh and unyielding, but the reassuring words "I will never leave you; or forsake you" were like a life insurance policy to me. I could face the future with confidence and peace, for God was my helper.

While praying and meditating on Hebrews 13:4–8, I began to realize why God wanted me to honor my marriage vows, why the relationship between husband and wife was so important to him. Firstly, it was important to honor a vow I had made. Early in the Garden of Eden, marriage was God's idea for man and woman to become one flesh, just as they are to be one with God. Second, God wants godly offspring, and godly offspring come from godly parents (who honor their vows). Third, how couples relate to one another establishes the emotional tone of the home, either loving and secure or stressful and conflictual, or somewhere in between. God wants his love to flow between parents and to pour his love onto their offspring. Above all, God wants children who love and honor him, following his purpose for their lives. I listened.

MY BRIDEGROOM

For as a young man marries a young woman, so shall your sons marry you, and as the bridegroom rejoices over the bride, so shall your God rejoice over you. (Isaiah 62:5)

For your Maker is your husband, the Lord of hosts is his name; and the Holy One of Israel is your Redeemer, the God of the whole earth he is called. (Isaiah 54:5)

In the process of rebirthing a new self, one surrendered to Jesus, I experienced a soul searching process of uncovering the pain and sin that led to this place. Facing the knowledge of GK's betrayal pulled the rug out from under me and the foundation of my former life crumbled. The pain and hurt I had swallowed deep inside, despite knowing the truth, erupted as a raw bleeding wound.

For several decades, I traveled down two paths simultaneously. My interest and study of psychology prompted me to delve into my childhood on a path of inner discovery, uncovering strengths and weaknesses, while also uncovering and resolving dysfunctional patterns. In my career, as well as my personal life, I experienced first-hand the impact of divorce on children, paying the price for their parents' inability to love one another. I advocated for the family. Often while counseling parents concerning parenting issues, problems due to marital difficulties emerged, and I faithfully offered strategies and resources to help resolve their problems knowing God hates divorce.

I was living a lie on the other path of my own married life. The Holy Spirit is not blind. By not dealing directly and effectively with signs of GK's infidelity when they first appeared, I became unwillingly compliant. Ignored sin only grows worse. Only when we shine God's light on sin and seek his healing are we being who God created us to be. I realized that only when we go beyond ourselves, lay our self-centered egos aside, and rely on the power of the Holy Spirit are we really being who God created us to be.

I thought back about the conversation Nicodemus, a member of the Jewish ruling council, had with Jesus one evening when Jesus told him no one can see the kingdom of God unless they are born again. When Nicodemus wondered how the old could be reborn, Jesus assured him he was referring to spiritual rebirth. God is spirit. Nicodemus immediately realized he could do nothing to be born again. Even as a respected teacher of the law, all his knowledge and great accomplishments were worthless. His hopes for eternal life were dashed. Nicodemus, like all of us, needed to come to the place of not trusting in his own righteousness, which seemed to be the typical perspective among the Pharisees. We all need to be emptied before God can fill us up. Recognizing the illusions and pretenses I had lived by forced me to shed the old self, laying my self-sufficiency, pride, and wounds at the feet of Jesus. This opened the way for God to release the transforming power of the Holy Spirit as "We are being changed into his likeness from one degree of glory to another" (2 Corinthians 3:18), rebirth by rebirth.

Whenever anyone turns to the Lord, the veil is taken away. The Lord is spirit, and there is freedom where the spirit of the Lord is. We all, who with unveiled faces contemplate the Lord's glory, are "are being transformed into the same image from one degree of glory to another" (2 Corinthians 3:18).

My thoughts delved into Jesus as my bridegroom, and I was the "Beloved" loved by Jesus. I let this transformative truth seep into my heart, mind, and will. Beloved is your truest identity. This is the reason wounds to the heart are so devastating. Sometimes while in prayer in the quiet of the early morning, I rested in the strong arms of Jesus, my Lord and Savior. Being dependent on Jesus is a place of serene security. His words, "Never will I leave you; Never will I forsake you" are a source of great joy and peace. As I progress through each day, Jesus is in me guiding and protecting me from mishaps and surprising me with blessings big and small.

> Fear not, for you will not be ashamed; be not confounded, for you will not be disgraced; for you will forget the shame of your youth, and the reproach of your widowhood you will remember no more. For your Maker is your husband, the LORD of hosts is his name; and the Holy One of Israel is your Redeemer, the God of the whole earth he is called. (Isaiah 54:4–5).

SEEING AND HEALING

Divorce turned GK's and my world upside down, forcing us to push past defense mechanisms and face the truth. In three years apart, we both grew closer to God. GK wrote numerous love letters. In one of these letters, he wrote,

> When I stood up for the Lord on August 16th, 1983, God started me on a journey that continues today, and will probably continue to the day I die. There has been some terrible pain in this journey, but that is no reason for sadness but rather for joy! I feel that God felt, in order to give me my recreation, he needed to humble me, completely strip me bare if you will, mentally, economically, spiritually. I need to confess my sins against you, my children, our children, and others. We can never be acceptable to God, but he could barely tolerate me! But humbling—this stripping my soul made me look back and see the horror of it all. And that is the great joy and happiness and glory that I feel. I can SEE.

A CONDUIT FOR GOD'S LOVE

The sacrifices of God are a broken spirit; a broken and contrite heart, O God, you will not despise. (Psalm 51:17)

We can never be a conduit for God's kindness and compassion to others until we recognize the sin and brokenness in our own lives. Sin is a fact of life. Sin is deliberate and determined independence from God, mutiny against God—either sin or God must die in our life. Jesus was crucified on the cross to pay for our sin debt. It is the only reason Jesus Christ came into this world and the reason for the sorrow and grief of life.

The New Testament presents a fundamental truth, which is—if sin rules in me, God's life in me will be killed. Yet if God rules in me, sin will be killed. Until coming to grips with your own sin, you will never be able to love yourself or others. Unfortunately for most of us, the path to this truth involves pain and suffering. We experience a transformation—our new humble and broken self emerges, newly realizing the magnitude of Jesus's sacrifice for us—his love, grace, and forgiveness. Only through acceptance we are imperfect and need God do we emerge as the bride of Christ—known and loved in the deepest parts of ourselves, having positioned our hearts under God's sovereignty, in humility. We can then genuinely treat others with the kindness and compassion that comes from the Lord, having been first-hand receivers of such tender care, knowing we are forever held.

> Embracing what God does for you is the best thing you can do for him. Don't become so well-adjusted to your culture that you fit into it without thinking. Instead, fix your attention on God. You'll be changed from the inside out. Readily recognize what he wants from you, and quickly respond to it. Unlike the culture around you, always dragging you down to its level of immaturity, God brings the best out of you, develops well-formed maturity in you (Romans:1–2).

A NEW PATH

After our divorce, GK moved to Wisconsin, and I remained in Connecticut. The house remained in my name. GK called every day, sometimes twice a day over a period of several years. I became very involved in my church, Bible study, and the women's covenant group. In my studies, I became increasingly interested in the latest research regarding family and parenting practices and how they correlated with biblical wisdom. Respect for how Jesus views the sanctity of marriage, cherished the importance of the family, hated divorce, and commanded forgivingness grew in my mind and soul.

Over time, GK and I grew closer, and our conversations became longer, deeper, more meaningful. During his weekend visits, not only did our conversations have more depth, but we laughed and enjoyed each other more. The love of Jesus was softening my heart. The words in the Lord's Prayer, "Forgive us our trespasses as we forgive others" pierced my conscience. Jesus was giving me a tender, forgiving heart.

While GK and I were attending church together one weekend in May, God put on my heart we were to be remarried in August. The wedding was to be a gathering of family and friends to celebrate the glory of God. Out of the ashes of our divorce, two people had grown closer to God, surrendering their lives to him.

The Flowers and the Wedding

August 16, 1986, a warm, sunny, Saturday afternoon, we were married at Saint Paul's Episcopal Church surrounded by friends and family. As the wedding quests sang hymns praising the Lord for his love and power, there was not a dry eye in the place. Hearts were warmed, witnessing the miracle of forgiveness and reconciliation. GK gave me an eternity ring, a circle of diamonds, symbolizing his love and pledge of unbroken faithfulness. The glory of the Lord was in this place.

God said our remarriage was to be a celebration, and it was a celebration. There were to be no gifts, only flowers. Trucks delivered bouquets all day to our home. By the end of the day of our wedding, every table in our home was filled with flowers. It was as if Eden had been ushered in again— the fragrance of flowers and beauty surrounded our story of love and redemption of love, redemption, forgiveness, and grace, pregnant with the promise to love each other again.

We held the reception at our home—a country French-style house nestled on two and a half acres rich in wildlife and foliage. All our friends who had hung with us over the years were there. During that period, we were in the best small group we had ever been in. It was a blessing to be surrounded by the love of that group—we all knew each other so well.

Cute little Haley, my first grandchild, was just three months old. Her fresh precious life was a symbol for this new love grown from what was, gifted anew—to cherish lifelong. That is just what we did.

Practices to Ponder

1. Are you honoring your marriage vows? If not, what needs to change?

2. Have you laid your self-sufficiency, pride, and wounds at the feet of Jesus?

3. In prayer together, ask Jesus to put on your heart the steps to take to cherish and nurture your marriage.

Prayer

Do not be anxious about anything, but in everything by prayer and supplication with thanksgiving let your requests be made known to God. And the peace of God, which surpasses all understanding, will guard your hearts and your minds in Christ Jesus. (Philippians 4:6–7)

—CHAPTER ELEVEN—
CULTIVATING CONNECTION

Two are better than one ... a threefold cord is not quickly broken. (Ecclesiastes 4:9–12)

GOD IS THE GLUE

Marriage is God's idea. "The LORD God said, 'It is not good for man should be alone. I will make him a helper fit for him'" (Genesis 2:18). In the marital union, couples form a partnership described in Scripture as becoming one flesh. Thus, the crowning achievement of creation was the holy union of man and woman. Only then did God declare it was good and rested from his work (Genesis 1:27–31).

The second time around, we realized just as Jesus is head of the church, he is also head of the family. I knew with the spirit of Jesus at the head of the household, love, respect, harmony, and forgiveness follow. GK and I were partners surrendering to the authority of Jesus. We knew Jesus would lead us in harmony. If we disagreed on major issues, we kept praying until God gave us a clear path. Relinquishing control and putting God in charge is a liberating experience. Sinful habits or reactions fall away upon drawing closer to Jesus. As we prayed together, our relationship became deeper and more meaningful, and what an amazing difference. Astonishing. God blessed our faith.

Keeping Christ at the head of your life and marriage requires daily, perhaps hourly, prayer to keep the lines open for God's love to flow through you. Jesus said, "If you abide in me, and my words abide in you, ask whatever you wish, and it will be done for you" (John 15:7). I have found the closer you are to God, the more loving and less selfish you become.

The goal of marriage is holiness, not happiness. Glorifying God by making both husband and wife more and more like Jesus begins with placing Jesus at the head of the household. Ephesians 4 says, "Rather, speaking the truth in love, we are to grow up in every way into him who is the head, into Christ" (v.15). Transforming your old self to the image of Christ doesn't erase the essence of who you are. Instead, by emulating Jesus, you develop into the unique person you were designed to be. As husband and wife grow closer to Jesus, they also become closer and more loving to each other.

Our home became a gathering place for love and fellowship. Bright and early every Monday morning, men gathered in our family room for Bible study, prayer, fellowship, coffee, and bagels or Danish. Our couples group met every Wednesday evening for prayer, guidance, fellowship, and Bible study.

TAKING YOUR EYE OFF GOD

We always face the choice of following Jesus or ourselves. Initially, GK relinquished control to God and was blessed by a miracle in his business dealings. With God's guidance, GK and a team of men acquired Cuisinart Inc., making GK the CEO. Unfortunately, over time, GK began making decisions his way rather than God's way. I noticed he started leaving the Monday men's prayer group early, then not attending at all, even though it was in our family room. He had taken his eye off God, forgetting the prayer group was his doing.

As a result, GK lost his position at Cuisinart, dealing him a financial and emotional blow as business circumstances quickly unraveled. At first, he was stunned, then angry. Gradually GK realized he had stopped listening to God, allowing his ego to get in the way. GK experienced enormous monetary loss caused by taking the reins of control from God and making decisions in his own power instead. Although he later became involved with some startups, GK had lost his stride and was never again employed at that level.

FAITHFUL

> Trust in the LORD with all your heart, and do not lean on your own understanding. In all your ways acknowledge him, and he will make straight your paths. (Proverbs 3:5–6; my [Jean's] life verse)

God was faithful. During this crisis, while praying, Jesus led me to the following passage:

> Fear not, for I am with you; be not dismayed, for I am your God; I will strengthen you, I will help you, I will uphold you with my righteous right hand. Behold, all who are incensed against you shall be put to shame and confounded; those who strive against you shall be as nothing and shall perish. You shall seek those who contend with you, but you shall not find them; those who war against you shall be as nothing at all. For I, the LORD your God, hold your right hand; it is I who say to you, "Fear not, I am the one who helps you. (Isaiah 41:10–13)

Praying together regularly, we found a new bond of intimacy—seeking God's wisdom, direction, and purpose for our lives. God still heals today as he did in the Bible. However, many of us do not receive his power because we are too busy running our own lives, lacking the necessary faith and discipline to walk intimately with God, seeking his healing.

If one dedicates a quiet time at the beginning of each day, praying, reading the Bible, and listening to God, wonderful things begin to happen.

FORGIVENESS IS ESSENTIAL

Be kind to one another, tenderhearted, forgiving one another, as God in Christ forgave you. (Ephesians 4:32)

By concentrating on God's love and grace we become gentler and kinder, less selfish, and critical. The process of finding one's true self begins with being broken, but faithful, in the presence of Jesus.

Knowing we have been forgiven and redeemed by our sweet Lord Jesus compels us to forgive others. Forgiveness is an essential form of love in relationships. Without it, built-up resentment against one another makes us bitter, preferring anger to restoration. Forgiving others is good for your mental health too. Loren Toussaint, Professor of Psychology at Luther College says, "If you don't have forgiving tendencies, you feel the raw effect of stress in an unmitigated way."[1] Researchers have found the quality of being highly forgiving of yourself and others nearly eliminates the connection between stress and mental illness.

SHARING STORIES

After our remarriage, my husband and I were always a part of a Christian couple's group. Gathering weekly, we shared our joys and problems, studied the Bible, and supported and prayed for each other. In sharing our stories with each other, we found common ground for healing, began to recognize the false self and true self in each other, and fought for the true self to come alive. We realized an intimacy, depth of insight, strength of community, and loving friendship on the deepest level.

GOD'S GUIDANCE

God wants us to come to him because of who he is. God's goal for us is making us like Jesus. As we become more like him, we discover our true selves, the persons he created us to be. The blessing of his presence brings incredible peace and joy, his encouragement brings us hope.

Upon retirement, we were torn between living on the East or the West Coast. We had taken many vacations exploring communities along the southeastern coastline. Our favorite was the Landings Club on Skidaway Island, a luxury, gated community located twelve miles from the historic city of Savannah. We both enjoyed golf and were history buffs, so it fit us like a tee (no pun intended). Some of our midwestern friends had already retired there.

On the other hand, my two sons, their families, and four grandchildren lived in California, so the pull there was strong. Looking up from prayer one day, GK suggested we should retire in California. "You are younger and healthier than I am. When I am gone, your sons will take care of you." The Lord led us to the perfect, private community, Coto de Caza, one of Orange County's oldest and most expansive master-planned communities with two eighteen-hole golf courses. While we were in prayer, Jesus even guided us to the perfect house.

Initially, we had selected a two-story house with four bedrooms, considering our kids and grandchildren. When we offered to buy the house, we were told we needed to enter the lottery that would be held in a month. During our tour of model homes, we viewed a smaller single-story home that GK commented, "Would be a great home for us when we are older." It was the very home God put on my heart. Later when GK was diagnosed with Parkinson's disease, we realized the wisdom of following Jesus once again.

Practices to Ponder

1. What are the steps I need to take to make Jesus head of the family?

2. Do I belong to a small group where sharing my story would help others?

3. Am I creating a life in Jesus and the Father that helps others to see grace in action?

Prayer

Lord help me to slow down and be present with you and others so I might truly see people with your eyes as you do.

—CHAPTER TWELVE—
AND THEY LIVED ... EVER AFTER

JESSICA AND ANDY

I cringe thinking back to our wedding and early marriage. Truly. Thinking of twenty-two-year-old me, looking out at the people gathered in a generous acquaintance's backyard where we were to have our ceremony in San Clemente, California, takes me back to a version of me that is not the person I am today. The girl looking out the window is so brave, yet so broken there—very insecure, standing in white, wearing a lot of makeup and a bad stick-on bra, and feeling a lot of confusion inside.

During the first years of our courtship and marriage, I was largely stuck in a dance of unhealthy concern with my family of origin and forging a new marriage and family without much support or blessing from my family. Andy was much more emotionally secure at that time than I was, but he was also very rough around the edges in the sense he felt no need to impress or charm my parents or brothers. This left my family thinking I'd made a life-ending decision, and me feeling pulled between two families.

Two weeks after our marriage, we moved to Hangzhou, China, where we lived for two years. They were the most adventure-filled years of my life and the most difficult years of our marriage. People have often said, "Wow, that must have been difficult living in China," and I'd think, *Not at all.* What was difficult was feeling the severance of love and understanding as the golden-daughter-turned-disappointment, rejected due to marrying. I was supposed to become a New York journalist or lawyer, not marry a southern boy with an accent, who sometimes doesn't wear a shirt and has no money. I very much felt my parents' disapproval of my choice in a spouse and life decisions, and this shattered me—the previously golden child.

I felt strongly he was God's match for me, but it was not easy or pretty. Our marriage was not a Hollywood happily-ever-after or like *Father of the Bride.* I felt stuck as a young girl inside a woman's body, a young wife caught between the devotion of her parents, family, and new husband. I realized, through sweat, blood, and tears, I would be forced to put one above the other. This separation did not happen easily but instead, like a large Chinese cleaver on a chicken's head, was abrupt and harsh, with a lot of blood and feathers flying every which way. This period of my life was particularly lonely, and I began feeling sorry for myself and regretful. Life would have been easier if we were like the ex-pats around us in the neighboring apartments—in their twenties, teaching English and living like celebrities, partying all over the city and making out with different people each week. I knew deep down that wasn't me, and I was smart enough to make my own choices, knowingly and committedly. Because something was strange to others or difficult was never a motivator for changing a decision. Only this time, stepping into the full weight of my life and decisions was lonelier than ever before.

At that point, I made a choice to re-devote myself to seeking God through his Word regularly, seeking fellowship with other believers, and looking honestly at myself and my past. During that time, I was dedicated to understanding my own anger and pain and distinguishing it from my surroundings. This initiated many years of work puzzling out the truth about all aspects of my life. I was finally open to becoming more of who God was calling me to be, and with the help and miracle of Jesus as the central head of our marriage, we began reworking our marriage piece by piece until it was an entirely new place of sanctuary and love.

THE CONTINUED JOURNEY

Andy and I are still very much on our marriage journey: married for thirteen years but happily married for about the last five, since starting to work on our marriage eleven years ago. I so wish joyful, put-together moments comprised the majority of our days. But, more often than not, our house is abustle with one child whining here, the other cutting a thousand snips of paper for a project, and one of us feeling scattered and scrambling, behind on the daily to-do list.

Andy and I still annoy each other. Our ongoing fight is centered on our different ways of communicating, very much rooted in what we observed growing up and have had to recognize and address. He tends to be a "I'll just suck it up" kind of guy, which, when he's irritated, can bring about passive aggressiveness and an angry, unloving tone. I am quick-tempered, which is very much a thorn in my flesh, and can quickly fluctuate between happy, fun-loving, and easy-going to hopeless and melancholic.

I tend to be unrelenting when talking things through, which is another area we've had to address and work through over the years. I drive Andy insane sometimes, asking him the same question many ways until I feel his answer is sufficient and fleshed out. He can drive me crazy with his methods of going about things, so different from my own approach. I find solace, however, in the fact that all marriages have such petty irritations and skirmishes, and those who don't perhaps ignore their feelings or don't communicate, which is a much greater cause for concern.

As individuals on their own separate journeys while living so close to each other, we cannot expect to continue growing closer to the Lord and not face continual conflict. This is especially true in rearing children and the hundreds of daily tasks and decisions that need to be made within the close and intimate quarters of marriage. But I think God calls us to continue to work out these issues as we follow him in the same direction in Christ. In my marriage, this compels me to see not through the lens of daily annoyances (and there are many) but rather through the bigger looking glass of Christ, where we get a more comprehensive view. In Jesus, we are required as believers to see through the lens of the bigger picture, the bigger story.

When Peter saw Jesus and began to walk toward him on the water, he began to sink when he looked away from the resurrected Jesus. It is the same with us. If we forget Jesus but for only a moment, our faith wanes quickly, and we find ourselves drowning. Marriage is very much like ocean waves in that sometimes the waters will be calm, the sun shining. At other times, we face unbelievable and sudden adversity and challenges and can lose our footing and barely see ahead. Yet, Jesus is the third strand of the chord which anchors us.

THE MARRIAGE I (JESS) DREAMED OF

She began now to comprehend that he was exactly the man who, in disposition and talents, would most suit her. His understanding and temper, though unlike her own, would have answered all her wishes. It was a union that must have been to the advantage of both: by her ease and liveliness, his mind might have been softened, his manners improved; and from his

judgment, information, and knowledge of the world,
she must have received benefit of greater importance.
—Jane Austen, *Pride and Prejudice*[1]

Andy was to be home at five, and after a long day with the
kids, I was eager for him to provide some relief with them. At
four-thirty, I was exhausted after a day of constant cleaning,
picking up after the kids' meals, my son crawling around
chairs and my legs all day, making appointments, changing
diapers, catching up on correspondence. The after-school
projects with my active and eager daughter included making
a fall paper pumpkin wreath and her reenacting her entire
preschool day playing "school" where she was the teacher
and I was the student, my infant son an unruly child in class.
Neither child had a nap other than my son, in the car, while
dropping his sister off. Feeling tired and lacking patience,
the last thirty minutes waiting for my husband's arrival felt
aggravating, bordering on anger, as exhaustion often feels.
The kids and I loaded up in the double stroller and headed
out to an area on campus where we are living that has herbs
and hot peppers for picking. Bella helped me pick cilantro
and green peppers, we picked lots of basil and said hellos
to passersby and neighbors on our walk home.

Andy arrived, and we were all thrilled to see him. He
began playing with the kids. "I just want to cook," I said.
He knew my look of "I need a break" and promptly took the
kids to take the trash out.

In my relief of quiet, I began chopping and sautéing garlic
and onions, taking in the comforting and invigorating aroma
of the peppers and herbs we had picked. Stirring in the leaves
of basil, I thought about how, over the years, I've realized
cooking really good food feeds my own soul. Cooking allows
me to connect with myself, and the Lord and I get caught
up in the fragrances of the food, creating something that
nourishes myself, my husband, and my kids.

We ate dinner amidst lots of requests from the kids, "more water," "another spoon," bits of good conversation, and lots more mess. As dinner finished, Andy said something funny and got up from his chair, acting silly. He took a pillow from the couch nearby and hit himself in the face with it. Bella laughed and Rocky got excited and began squealing too. Lots of laughter, and Bella got up and began copying her dad's silly actions. Giggling and wrestling ensued. I smiled and tried to capture this moment in my mind, trying to create an indelible picture of this moment: happiness amidst the chaos of real life. In my heart, I recognized the fulfillment of an answer to many years of prayer—for more levity, more laughter, more ease and joy in my life, in my marriage, for my children. The prayer of having a Christ-centered marriage has been answered—of having a life partner who is a true and loyal friend.

THE BLESSING OF BEING KNOWN

My husband has invested years getting to know me. Andy knows my quirks, my ways, my soul. He supports my dreams and my down time. He respects me. He wants to provide for and protect me. And I feel contented in his company. My most comfortable place is with him, my cherished partner in this life.

We have a shared investment in our children—a shared partnership in all aspects of childrearing and the home. There has not been one time in the night, when awakened by one of our young kids crying, Andy has not woken too. Our daughter often calls out for Andy in the night if she is scared, and he willingly comforts her.

Over the last eleven years of marriage, we have figured out our strengths and allowed those to rise. Andy doesn't mind dishes, so he's the home washer of all things dish. I love homemaking and shopping and don't mind vacuuming.

We've gotten into a rhythm, which was clunky in our

early marriage but smooth now where no topic is unworthy or too painful to discuss. We've talked about our deepest sorrows and our greatest dreams. We've shared our embarrassingly painful moments and have experienced together our greatest joys. We are intensely aware of each other's feelings and those of our children and work hard to acknowledge and care for them. We share a life of adventure.

We pray for ourselves, for our family, for each other, for our leaders, for policy, for the underprivileged, for our world. We have found separate interests and friends, as well as joined interests. We've worked hard to establish healthy boundaries with our extended families for the health of ourselves and our children and boundaries with each other, recognizing our valued separateness. We've also learned to practice making our default answer "no," reserving our "yes" for those things we value most, knowing time is a valuable and limited resource and that we need to be good stewards of it.

Practices to Ponder

1. What pains in the past are waiting to be acknowledged and grieved?

2. How much of my avoidance of difficult issues is driven by a need to be liked?

3. Are you learning to bring up a problem using "I" statements without attacking or belittling?

4. Are you doing anything that soothes your anxiety but betrays your integrity?

5. Is your spouse your best friend? If not, how can you strengthen this relationship?

Prayer

Did he not make them one, with a portion of the Spirit in their union? And what was the one God seeking? Godly offspring. So guard yourselves in your spirit, and let none of you be faithless to the wife of your youth. (Malachi 2:15)

—CHAPTER THIRTEEN—
BARRIERS

Getting married is a risky business. In the marriage relationship, we often experience our greatest joy and deepest despair. Yet most of us want, with all our heart, to have a loving marriage. A loving marriage provides the optimum environment to raise children.

REFINING TIES WITH PARENTS

When a couple marries, their first task is separating from the family of origin, to invest fully in the marriage. At the same time, it is necessary to refine their relationships with both sets of parents. This is especially difficult for many mothers and daughters because the ties are so strong. Many marriages never achieve true intimacy because the primary lines of communication continue between mother and daughter rather than between husband and wife. "Therefore a man [woman] shall leave his father and mother and hold fast to his wife [her husband], and the two shall become one flesh" (Ephesians 5:31). Being one flesh does not mean God purées you together in a blender. Rather each spouse is called into partnership with God to deliver his love, truth, and encouragement in becoming who God designed you to be.

AND THEY LIVED ...

Unfortunately, all too often, the radiance of the bridal procession pales as couples struggle to forge an intimate partnership while retaining individual integrity. More than half of all marriages result in divorce. Why is it difficult for many couples to develop an intimate, loving union? Why is tender, loving care so hard to find?

Before choosing a mate, one first must be able to stand alone. The further along each partner is in the process of becoming their unique authentic self, the more available they are to form a loving, lasting union. A partner who enters marriage without a solid identity enters the union emotionally crippled. In marriage, independent identities of both partners need to be viewed in terms of what is best for each person while considering the health of the marriage.

The developmental task of adulthood, according to Erik Erickson, involves emotional separation from the family of your childhood and forging a new identity.[1] This means making your own decisions, establishing an independent stance, and being able to rely on your own moral judgment. This also means being financially independent. Most of us marry without these abilities, relying on our partner to fill in where we haven't developed ourselves.

The barriers to forming loving relationships are many, and counterfeits to love abound. We all bring unaddressed and unhealed psychological baggage from the past into our marriages. If a person needs more from the partnership than the strengths he or she brings to the marriage, the intensity of these needs will burden, or at worst strangle, the relationship.

Why is it so difficult to truly love one another? Distorted values in our culture today promote an immoral, narcissistic lifestyle—if it feels good, looks good, and I want it, then I should have it. The myth of romantic love, fed by Hollywood, perpetuates a lie, which seriously undermines many relationships. Adults and children alike are being brainwashed watching various versions of this myth. Thus, the expectations that "being in love" is one of our inalienable rights, becomes the source of much unhappiness, providing the motivation or justification for changing partners and destroying families.

Many people naively think marriage will solve all their problems. The expectation our mates should meet all our needs and demands renders disappointment when they cannot deliver. Frustration is inevitable if we expect our mates to meet our every longing. Everyone loses when one attempts to dominate or control the other. Sometimes both dance to the tune of their injured child within, driven by self-centered desires or distorted perceptions. Marital harmony quickly vanishes. Some turn from their spouse to pursue happiness with another led on by the popular Hollywood myth an individual's basic right to pursue happiness includes one wonderful exhilarating experience after another. As time passes, they come to realize they have recycled the problem rather than resolved it, never fully realizing they are the one person responsible for their happiness.

Self-centeredness and selfishness create a lot of pain and conflict in intimate relationships. When two self-centered individuals marry, storm clouds quickly gather and the battle between individual ways erupts. Children are self-centered—just watch a group of preschool children to see the "me first" attitude in action. Children need to be taught how to share and compromise, considering the needs of others in addition to their own. Empathy must be taught and modeled. Unfortunately, some of us have reached adulthood without learning this lesson.

Love as Feelings

Many think of love as a feeling. and as soon as one's feelings dampen, one seeks a new source of sunshine. Feelings, like the weather, change. One moment it's sunny, the next stormy. In one season it's hot, the next it isn't. In this climate, the emotional temperature of a marriage changes like the weather.

Although love is not based on feelings alone, one's feelings need to be acknowledged and addressed. Your convictions, which for Christians align with the Scripture, are determined by facts. Facts and feelings need to walk hand-in-hand with open communication and vulnerability. Confronting negative emotions is the beginning of understanding. It is human either to be led by our emotions or to live solely in the world of reasoning and facts, denying one's emotions. As always, balance is best.

Cycle of Negativity

Gottman found for a marriage to last, there must be at least five positive interactions for every negative one. Fondness and admiration are two crucial elements in a rewarding and long-lasting romance. Fondness and admiration are also crucial for friendship—the core of any good marriage. Without the fundamental belief that your spouse is worthy of honor and respect, where is the basis of any kind of rewarding relationship? Nurture your fondness and admiration.

Although we all lose our temper at times, a continuing pattern of conflict is extremely damaging to all concerned. In researching his book, *Staying the Course*, an examination of the careers and marriages of eighty successful men, Robert Weiss, psychology professor at the University of Massachusetts, found the impact of domestic disputes is severe. "It just lays people out," he wrote, "if you go on hurting each other and tearing each other apart, be careful, or you will completely destroy each other"[3]

JUDGMENT

When problems arise in marital relationships, it is human to paint oneself as wise and witty, while planning massive reconstruction of one's mate. This isn't helpful although a common practice. Why? It distracts you from uncovering your own role in perpetuating the problem.

The Bible warns Christians against being judgmental. Many marital problems are caused by one or both spouses being critical of the other, pointing out minor incidents while overlooking major problems in their own behavior. The book of Matthew chapter seven supports this when it says, "Why do you see the speck that is in your brother's eye, but do not notice the log that is in your own eye?" (v. 3).

AN ATTITUDE OF UNFORGIVENESS

Holding grudges and refusing to forgive our partners is a roadway to destroying relationships. Harboring resentment damages both partners, causing conflict and stress. We have all heard the expression, "Don't get mad, get even." This attitude of revenge stirs up more anger and hurtful behavior, thus exacerbating the problem. The revenger and victim are both consumed with negative hurtful emotions. The desire for revenge can be exceedingly destructive. Rather, noticing anger as a sign that a change needs to take place is constructive.

My (Jean's) background in psychology helped me to be sensitive and see my husband's hurtful behavior not so much as a personal attack but the result of his own pain and shame from his own internal feelings. Gaining such a sensitivity allows one to separate the person from the problem, enabling one to hate the problem and not the person. This lays the groundwork for a more forgiving attitude. This growth also helped me keep perspective and not accept the sinful behavior, which was keeping us from having a close, open, and trusting relationship. Our relationship could only be rightly restored after growing from scratch. It took a separation, divorce, and separate healing and boundaries for our relationship to grow in the Lord.

Too many couples move from hurt to "forgiveness" too quickly, without addressing anything. This happens either because they cannot withstand the work of confronting issues one by one, or because they want to pretend everything is okay and "back to normal." While seemingly kind, these responses to hurt are selfish desires—wanting to feel okay more than wanting to really make things whole and restored in Christ. This does not help anyone become more godly or more focused on Christ's truth or redeeming power.

Let's consider the analogy of a home that needs a deep cleaning. If instead of cleaning well, things are pushed into closets and brushed under the couch—is the house truly clean or is the mess just in a state of dirty pretend?

Immature couples often have too much denial involved, with more and more hurt stacking up until the relationship is characterized only by hurt or denial. Neglecting to regularly address issues causes a lack of genuine connection.

Forgiveness is essential in all relationships. We are all sinners who, thoughtlessly or deliberately, take actions that hurt others. For some, the desire to keep voluminous records of wrongs done to them prevents them from moving forward. Whenever I am tempted to hang on to a hurt, the Lord's Prayer comes to mind, "Forgive us our trespasses as we forgive others." We need to discern which issues are worth fighting for, using the strength of God to understand how to love through the fight.

Dr. Dan B. Allender, in his text *Bold Love*, discusses the temptation to forget God is good even when the earth is fallen, and relationships can be very hurtful and discouraging. He says:

> God does not seem to show his goodness to those who peer through the lens of a skeptical examiner or a demanding negotiator. The Evil One uses the pain and confusion of a fallen world to shadow doubt over God's goodness. As long as the laughter of being forgiven is silenced by the somber tones of doubt and anger, God's goodness will be shrouded in the darkness of this world. Forgiveness is the light that penetrates the dark and frees the somber, shamed heart to leap with love.[4]

While forgiveness is essential and needs to be continual for relationships to flourish, it is anything but easy or simple. The adage "forgive and forget" does not work and, in fact, is not biblical. Forgiveness accompanies remembrance, consequences, redemption, and, ultimately, freedom. Dr. Allender further says,

> Forgiveness also involves a heart that cancels debts but does not lend new money until repentance occurs. A forgiving heart opens the door to any who knock, but entry into the home (that is, the heart) does not occur until the muddy shoes and dirty coat have been taken off. Offenders must repent if true intimacy and reconciliation are ever to occur. That means that cheap forgiveness—peace-at-any-cost that sacrifices honesty, integrity, and passion—is not true forgiveness.[5]

Forgiveness is serious business and is challenging to get right. Not only is confrontation difficult in general, but it is not easy to think clearly and logically about what forgiveness means or to understand how to walk in it with boldness and courage when we are hurt by those whom we love most.

A large and often undiscussed aspect of forgiveness is setting parameters and being open to the point of risking great loss. When we are transparent and vulnerable, while also setting boundaries and offering forgiveness, we achieve deeper relationships and connections, growing in love and maturity. We find offering forgiveness and redemption is a cherished gift and receiving forgiveness provides the greatest sense of love, peace: relief in knowing we are loved in our imperfection.

PRACTICES TO PONDER

1. How is God bringing you closer to him through difficulties and setbacks in your life?

2. Is there someone in your life today you need to ask for forgiveness? Be specific.

3. Are you learning to resolve conflict maturely by being quiet, listening, and considering the perspective of others?

4. Do you respect the parameters of others and ask for the parameters you need to live out your authentic self?

PRAYER

Put on then, as God's chosen ones, holy and beloved, compassionate hearts, kindness, humility, meekness, and patience, bearing with one another and, if one has a complaint against another, forgiving each other; as the Lord has forgiven you, so you also must forgive. And above all these put on love, which binds everything together in perfect harmony. (Colossians 3:12–14)

—CHAPTER FOURTEEN—
WISDOM TESTED

My son [daughter], do not forget my teaching, but let your heart keep my commandments, for length of days and years of life and peace they will add to you. (Proverbs 3:1–2)

GOD CUSTOMIZED ME (JEAN)

We moved into our new house in Coto de Caza, California, on July 4th, 1999. Our house in New Canaan had been a custom French country house. While surveying our new home, everywhere I looked, I saw possibilities for enhancement and embellishment—moldings, window treatments, wood cabinets, bookshelves—the list went on and on. After playing golf and decorating for the first year of our retirement, I still had many projects in mind. But when I heard a school district nearby was looking for school psychologists, I sent my résumé. During the interview, I explained I was customizing a tract house, would work a two-day week, and would only be there for two or three years.

What I intended as a lark, God intended as a lifeline. As GK's Parkinson's disease took a turn for the worse, my earnings not only customized a tract house but, more importantly, financed an ever-expanding need for the help of a caregiver. This income secured my future financial wellbeing, but there were psychological benefits as well because my career has always been therapeutic for me. Being involved with teachers, parents, and children throughout the day took my mind off my own problems, giving me fresh perspectives and renewed energy when addressing my own situation.

BATTLING PARKINSON'S DISEASE

> We call it forgiveness when we've moved on, but I think forgiveness is when you let tenderness move in. —Ruth Chou Simmons, *Gracelaced*[1]

This morning while praying in my backyard, I glanced upon a garden stone that reads, "GK 75th Birthday, Aged to Perfection." This stone commemorates the Last Hurrah, an al fresco dinner party celebrating GK's seventy-fifth birthday. What followed was the slow, steady deterioration of GK's health.

His balance was compromised first. Every Tuesday morning at a prompt six fifteen, GK's friend, Bill, would pick him up to attend a men's prayer group at Saddleback Church. One morning an irritated Bill called, demanding: "Where is GK?" Knowing GK had gone outside, I threw on a robe and dashed outside to find GK lying on the ground unable to get up. A visit to the emergency room determined GK had broken his elbow. Thus began eight years of broken bones, trips to the emergency room, and debilitating pain and suffering.

Parkinson's is a horrible disease, invading the mind as well as the body. Dealing with this disease felt like watching someone die one step at a time. GK fought every step of the way—fighting to remain upright rather than succumbing to a wheelchair, fighting to stay involved with others as his mind betrayed him, fighting to hang on to the pleasures of life. We had a tradition of going out to dinner every Friday night. I knew this was important to GK even though a challenge for me. Dressing an adult is a lot more difficult than dressing a baby, and that was just the beginning. Several times, we ordered our meal at a restaurant only for GK to become so ill we would need to leave, taking our meal as a carry-out.

Gradually, as GK's symptoms grew worse, additional help became a necessity. Following several attempts to find the appropriate caregiver, God brought us Gabbie, a handsome Christian man from the Philippines who came to the United States to support his family. Gabbie's availability complemented my work schedule, as he was not available on weekends or after six p.m. I continued working to defray the added cost of Gabbie's wages. God has a sense of humor. When I retired the second time, I was working a four-day week and had worked ten years.

These were very difficult days. GK was on hospice for six years. Over time, a hospital bed was ordered. Although GK could barely walk or see, somehow, even with the sides of the bed up, he would manage to get up in the wee hours of the night, stumble out of our bedroom, and fall in the foyer. The thump would wake me. I was not strong enough to lift him, so I called the fire department.

Late one Sunday afternoon, two weeks before Christmas, I had been caring for GK all weekend. I felt caged in and needed a break to get outside for a short walk. Making GK comfortable in a high back chair with his feet on an ottoman, remote in hand, and a Coke on the table beside him, I cautioned him to please remain seated as I would be back in fifteen or twenty minutes, and then, we could share a drink and have a nice dinner. Like a little kid, his mischievous nature took over as GK made other plans. When I returned from my walk, there was GK lying on the floor of the kitchen in front of the liquor cabinet. What could I do? I called the fire department.

This time things were different. The fire chief checked my record, discovering I had called the fire department thirty-six times that year—I was charged with overusing the fire department. This ended any help from the fire department. Gabbie, too, was realizing GK needed a higher level of care, and recommended a home care facility in a neighboring community. Reluctantly, I agreed. GK was in the caregiving residence for ten months, longing to come home. I visited him every day after work. God was faithful. Time passed, the school year ended, and Gabbie was available once again—I was able to bring GK home.

GK peacefully went to heaven on August 18, 2011.

LOVE REALIZED

In the eight years that I took care of GK before he lost his battle with Parkinson's disease, we kept up our tradition of sharing a drink, GK's version of an Old Fashioned for him and a glass of wine for me, followed by a nice dinner on Friday nights. When GK could no longer go out to eat, I found up-scale restaurants that delivered. In our conversations, he enjoyed hearing my stories about teachers, parents, and kids finding these topics more interesting than the "widgets" he sold. Despite all we had gone through, we managed to realize a true love and companionship with one another.

CELEBRATING GK'S LIFE

Love is creative and redemptive. Love builds up and unites; hate tears down and destroys. The aftermath of the 'fight with fire' method ... is bitterness and chaos, the aftermath of the love method is reconciliation and creation of the beloved community. —Martin Luther King, Jr.[2]

In hindsight, I realize I had become increasingly aware over the years that obeying God's guidance in Hebrews 13:4–8 to obey my marriage vows was a pivotal decision that impacted the rest of my life. First and foremost, mercy and forgiveness require a willingness to forget offenses and approach others with a tender heart.

During the celebration of GK's life, I gained further insight on why God wanted us to forgive one another, remarry, and live in harmony. I realized the ending of our lives really matters when I heard my sons Tom and Michael fondly recall how GK had coached their Little League games, attended football games, and taken keen interest in their business careers. The grandkids often comment about GK's quick wit and creative endeavors like how he even played drums in my grandson Jonathan's band. Our family is united by fond memories of GK, which continue to live with us today, all of us having witnessed the power of the Holy Spirit and God's love and forgiveness in our reconciliation and remarriage.

Not only is forgiveness good for relationships, but it's good for your health too. According to a study from the American Psychological Association, forgiving yourself and others can protect against the impact stress has on your mental health.[3]

Because of my decision to follow that gentle whisper of God shared by my mentor long ago, my faith grew, and my life was enriched. In every moment of every day, I am bathed in the love of Jesus and wrapped in a shield of protection. Had I not obeyed the voice, my family would have been left with a pile of broken pieces.

A NEW CALLING

One Sunday shortly after GK's death, Pastor Rick Warren, founding pastor of Saddleback Church in Lake

Forest, California, introduced a new series, "The Decade of Destiny."[4] During his sermon, he commented, "No matter how old you are, God has a purpose for you."

Encouraged by the sermon and while praying, thoughts of a new chapter in my life came to me. Now that I was neither married nor working, I decided then to dedicate the remainder of my life completely to Jesus, wanting him to be the focus of every day. It was then I heard the gentle voice, "The Book." I knew immediately what it meant. Years before, in graduate studies, my passion was to write a dissertation on how optimal child rearing practices correlated with biblical wisdom. At the University of Connecticut, a public university, the Bible was not held in high regard as a major resource. I became discouraged, chucked the whole idea, and slammed shut the four-drawer file filled with my research.

When we moved, GK asked, "Are you going to move that metal file cabinet clear across the country?" I pleaded, "Humor me, after all the time and effort I put into that project—it would be like leaving one of the boys behind." We hauled the files across the country to where they sat in our garage, untouched for years.

A MIRACLE

Responding to the gentle whisper of Jesus, I asked my son Michael, who was a television agent at that time, to pray about God's guidance for the book. Several weeks later, Michael called saying, "I don't usually mention you in business meetings, Mom, but I was talking to Shannon Marven, Executive Vice President, Dupree Miller & Associates, who is a sweet old lady like you. I told her about your book. She said, 'Send me what you have. I will have time to read it over the weekend.'" At first, I protested. I wasn't ready, but Michael would hear none of it, saying when opportunity knocks, go for it.

Within a few weeks, Shannon replied, "Your mom has done the research. You can tell she has been talkin' the talk and walkin' the walk for a long time. For me, the hook of the book is when your mom writes: 'A child that feels loved and understood is immeasurably easier to discipline than one who doesn't.'" Thus began the long process, with the help of ghostwriter Jeanette Thomason, of writing my first book. Following a series of miracles, delays, rewrites, and periods of waiting, *Purposeful Parenting: Six Steps to Bring Out the Best in Your Kids*[5] was published on May 15, 2015.

PRACTICES TO PONDER

1. What might be one way you can let go of control and choose to serve someone in love today?

2. What are some unhealthy attachments, idols, or addictions Jesus wants you to purge from your life to lead you to a closer relationship with him?

3. What problem in your life has resulted in the greatest growth of character?

PRAYER

Because he holds fast to me in love, I will deliver him; I will protect him, because he knows my name. When he calls to me, I will answer him; I will be with him in trouble; I will rescue him and honor him. With long life I will satisfy him and show him my salvation. (Psalm 91:14–16)

—CHAPTER FIFTEEN—
GUIDED BY LOVE

THE GREATEST COMMANDMENT

"Teacher, which is the great commandment in the Law?" And he said to him, "You shall love the Lord your God with all your heart and with all your soul and with all your mind. This is the great and first commandment. And a second is like it: You shall love your neighbor as yourself." (Matthew 22:36–39)

It is no wonder God instructed us to first love God, then love each other. Without knowledge of his Word and access to his power, there is no hope for success. Love is Jesus's top priority. Shortly before his time of suffering and crucifixion, Jesus said to his disciples, "A new commandment I give to you, that you love one another: just as I have loved you, you also are to love one another. (John 13:34).

GOD DEFINES LOVE

The apostle Paul defines love in the famous paragraph, 1 Corinthians 13:4–8. Paul describes love in behavioral terms, implying there is a choice:

Love is patient.
Love is kind.

Love does not envy.

Love does not boast.

Love is not proud.

Love does not dishonor others.

Love is not self-seeking.

Love is not easily angered.

Love keeps no records of wrongs.

Love does not delight in evil.

Love rejoices with the truth.

Love always protects.

Love always trusts.

Love always hopes.

Love always perseveres.

Love never fails.

Read these words first as God loves you. For example: God is patient, God is kind, God is not easily angered, and keeps no record of wrongs. Now turn the words around to reflect how you treat others—these are likely as apparent in our relations with others.

Recently, I (Jean) read *Image Heaven* by best-selling author John Burke, pastor and founder of Gateway Church in Austin, Texas, who has studied near-death experiences of thousands of survivors. The alignment of near-death experiences and Scripture is powerful, as is the exhilarating picture of heaven. Virtually all the stories involved direct contact with God or Jesus in a heavenly setting. Each of them gives the sense God is truly loving and wants you to realize how good and perfect his love is, that it is all we need. What impacted me most profoundly were the two questions Jesus inquired of all survivors, believers and non-believers alike. The first question was, "How did you love those people I brought into your life?" and the second, "How did you use the gifts, talents, and abilities you were given?"[1] Nothing else matters, not your career, your achievements, not how much money you earned, only how you loved others and used your gifts for God's purpose. These questions address walking in the spirit. Receiving Jesus as your Lord and Savior assures your salvation but doesn't always assure you are being loving or following God's guidance.

BEING FILLED WITH GOD'S LOVE

Only in complete surrender and oneness with Jesus Christ can the Holy Spirit flow through us. This requires a humble, contrite heart and a spirit saturated in the Word of God. It seems obvious if God is the source of love, then spending time in his presence and absorbing his Scripture is how to become more loving. I realize this to be true. Over the last forty years of spending at least thirty minutes a day alone with Jesus, I have slowly and unknowingly become less selfish and more generous, smiling more, joy and peace replacing worry and anxiety in my heart and soul. I've received not an exterior facelift, but an internal makeover.

Keeping the selfish self out of our relationships is closely related to how much we clothe ourselves in the righteousness of God and how much the presence of Jesus has purified our heart. These directly correlate to how much time we spent in his presence and his Word. The reference point of love is our foundation in Jesus, letting his love and character define you.

Oswald Chambers writes, "Jesus said, 'When he, the Spirit of truth, has come … He will glorify Me …' (John 16:13–14). When I commit myself to the revealed truth of the New Testament, I receive from God the gift of the Holy Spirit, who then begins interpreting to me what Jesus did.

The Spirit of God does for me internally all that Jesus Christ did for me externally."[2]

First, love is considerate. It is patient and kind (1 Corinthians 13:4). Therefore, reactions of frustration, irritation, and impatience should be kept at bay. As we treat others with a spirit of gentleness and graciousness, despite their treatment of us, we look for ways to be gracious and helpful.

Second, Christlike love is unselfish. Attitudes and actions rooted in self-interest or self-importance, such as jealousy, arrogance, self-entitlement, seeking one's own rights, easily provoked anger, and holding grudges are all driven by self-interest and therefore contrary to being unselfish. For many of us, most marital arguments are fueled by selfish demands and expectations.

Third, genuine love is discerning. True love is not blind. Truth and love do not exist in opposition but in perfect unity. Affirming or overlooking someone's sinful lifestyle or choices is not in their best interests and therefore not an act of love. Addictions of all kinds fall into this category, impacting marital and parental relationships. Addictive behavior must be confronted in love, out of a discerning, loving heart.

Fourth, love, according to apostle Paul in I Corinthians, endures. Love bears, believes, hopes, and endures all things (13:7). Despite outstanding circumstances, true love is grounded in faith and hope. As the old saying goes, love covers a multitude of sins, with the goal of restoration, not condemnation. The divorce rate in Orange County, California, where I live is at 68 percent. Despite a strong Christian message and an affluent environment, marriages crumble at this alarming rate.

Often, we try hard to love others but fail because our love is not yet a fruit of the Spirit. Jesus's spirit produces love as we surrender our lives to Jesus and live obediently. Like branches bearing fruit, his love flows through us to others.

MAKING LOVE LAST

Both partners desire and need love and respect. When we think of each other as unique individuals created in God's image, there is no room for disrespect or for one partner to dominate the other. In my water aerobics class, there is a couple, Bob and Joy, who have been married more than sixty years. They live attuned, anticipating each other's need, and providing help with a smile. I inquired of the reason for their long, loving relationship. They both said, in harmony, "Respect." John M. Gottman found in his extensive research regarding marriage that couples with greater emotional intelligence are better able to understand, honor, and respect each other, keeping their relationship positive.[3]

According to Gottman, happy marriages are based on a deep friendship, including mutual respect and enjoyment of each other's company. These couples tend to know each other intimately, each well versed in the other's likes, dislikes, hopes, and dreams. "The determining factor in whether wives feel satisfied with the sex, romance, and passion in their marriage is, by 70 percent, the quality of the couple's friendship. For men, the determining factor is, by 70 percent, the quality of the couple's friendship. So men and women come from the same planet after all." If you can say of your husband, "My lover, my best friend" your marriage is on solid ground.[4]

Good marriages provide a safe place for conflict. In any close intimate relationship, conflict is inevitable. While researching thousands of relationships, Gottman's team found all marital conflict falls into two categories—resolved or perpetual. Sixty-nine percent falls into the perpetual category, encompassing things like Joan is organized and neat regarding housework, while her husband Bill is absent-minded, organizes in piles, and frequently misplaces his keys, workout shoes, etc. Differences like these can become problematic if they remain unresolved, becoming sources of anger, and potentially pushing couples toward divorce. Couples in good marriages haven't necessarily solved their problems but have instead learned to live with them in a humorous and good-natured manner.

Love: A Choice and Commitment

The family of a wise woman lives in his light, and truth is the byproduct. Knowing the truth about how who you are in Christ impacts your identity is essential if you are to become a new creation. Jesus said, "If you abide in my word, you are truly my disciples, and you will know the truth, and the truth will set you free" (John 8:31–32).

Love is a choice and commitment. With commitment comes trust. Nothing so quickly dissolves intimacy as a betrayal of confidence. Only in an environment of trust, commitment, and vulnerability can true love flourish. Choosing true love is putting others first. An attitude of "my way or the highway" destroys intimacy and love. "Do nothing from selfish ambition or conceit, but in humility count others more significant than yourselves ... Have this mind among yourselves, which is yours in Christ Jesus" (Philippians 2:3–5). You are painting a picture of God's love in action if your attitude and words convey the message that your needs are important to me, that you deserve my love, respect, and attention. We get transformation when vulnerability and truth meet grace.

Practice the Holy Habit:
Thirty Minutes a Day Rule

One of the first identifiable love practices that helps couples stay connected seems so obvious—spending time together. Not watching television or playing computer games, text messaging, or being distracted by social media, but one-on-one time together with your undivided attention. This may sound simple enough but focusing on one another is increasingly difficult in these times of multitasking, with our attention constantly pulled in every direction. Perhaps the most important calling of our times is learning to discern and drown out the unimportant noise and turn up the two or three songs that really matter—the ones essential for our hearts, our lives, our marriages, and our children.

Be intentional. One-on-one time simply delighting in one another, listening to one another, sharing the concerns of the day, feelings behind the scenes. The Bible uses the word "delighting" to describe the way God loves us, his children. To me, delighting is love in action. Often sharing small talk daily keeps the circuits open. Are we relating to one another as good friends? Fondness and admiration are crucial to the friendship at the core of good marriages. One needs to learn to express thoughts and feelings, communicating openly and transparently—How are we doing? What do you need? Are we staying connected? Are we enjoying each other's company?

Spend time with your spouse, but also show them how you value and esteem their special talents and virtues. Ask about your spouse's goals, passions, and dreams and help them achieve these goals. Above all, make each other feel appreciated and cherished. Describe to them what you love about them. For example, "When I come home, I love it when you stop what you are doing and give me a big hug and welcoming smile."

Often at the end of the day I see couples happily walking their dog or baby in a carriage through the neighborhood, sharing their news and concerns of the day. As empty nesters, my husband and I enjoyed playing nine holes of golf together toward the end of the day. Often, we had the course to ourselves, reveling in the beauty of our surroundings and the company of each other.

While rereading Jess's description of how she and Andy relate to one another, I felt it was worth repeating how two people who love Jesus and one another will go through the pain of transformation to become "one flesh." To reiterate Jess's quote:

> We've gotten into a rhythm which was clunky in our early marriage but smooth now, where no topic is unworthy or too deep, personal, or painful to discuss. We've talked about our deepest sorrows and our greatest dreams. We've shared our embarrassingly painful moments as well as have experienced together, our greatest joys. We are intensely aware of each other's feelings and those of our children and work hard to acknowledge and care for them. We share a life of deep friendship, partnership, parenting, romance, and adventure.

BIMONTHLY OR MONTHLY CHECK-IN

1. Do each of you have a daily quiet time of solitude with God—praying, reading the Bible, and meditating on scripture?

2. Do you feel loved, cherished, and respected?

3. How is the balance of household responsibilities?

4. Are you happy with your romantic sexual intimacy?

5. Are you observing the Holy Habit, thirty-minute per day rule for time together?

6. Are you observing the rules for conflict resolution?

Second, concentrate on current problems and concerns. Instead of attacking problems in the heat of the moment, write down the source of your upset to provide a parking garage for your emotions, thus giving you time to pray and seek God's guidance and direction. Because the source is written down, both people have time to pray, think, and reflect on the issue before discussing the matter. This leads to a more thoughtful, reasoned response. Ask yourselves— are we holding ourselves accountable for the goals we agreed on? Why or why not?

BEING PREPARED

Before scheduling the Monthly Check-in, be careful to choose an appropriate time and place, as some of the topics may be sensitive. Avoid "you" (finger pointing) statements as they focus the blame on your partner, not the problem, and instead use "I" statements, sharing your thoughts and feelings. Establishing some ground rules for the Check-in before you begin is helpful. Rules help promote healthy discussion and deal with conflict constructively within a caring and loving framework.

1. Identify and focus on the problem.
2. Attack the problem not the person.
3. Listen with an open mind.
4. Treat your partner's feelings with respect.
5. Take responsibility for your own actions.

ACTIVE LISTENING

For most of us, listening is much harder than talking. Too often, we aren't listening to one another. At times, we are so focused on getting our point across we don't really listen and reflect on what the other person is saying. This is particularly true if emotions are running high. In this media-filled world, many are becoming "speed listeners" flooded with information. They impatiently hear only the lead, missing the details and emotional implications of what is being said.

There are three components of active listening—expressing verbal and nonverbal interest in what the person is saying, paraphrasing, and asking the person to elaborate. Begin by giving your spouse or partner the floor without interruption. Don't be judgmental or allow your own feelings to muddle your attention. The goal is to understand and relate to what the other person says regarding their feelings, their truth, and their story. Maintain good eye contact and give small indications of your listening such as "I see" or "Yes," or a nod of your head. When your partner is finished, reflect back what was said by summarizing, paraphrasing, or asking them to elaborate if you need further clarification. Using these techniques along with a soft calm voice and occasional smile will go a long way to encourage good communication in your marriage and to resolve conflict.

QUIZ: HOW WELL DO YOU KNOW YOUR SPOUSE?

1. What do they enjoy doing for fun or relaxation?
2. What is worrying them and causing stress?
3. What do they need your help with?
4. What do they want in the bedroom?
5. What do they secretly wish for?

SUPPORTED BY OTHERS

Enjoying each other and having good friends to socialize with increases happiness as a couple. Surround yourselves with godly couples who have strong marriages. Be deliberate about forging friendships with others who live out their commitment and faith in God.

Seek godly counsel. When you hit a roadblock, it is often helpful to seek the wisdom of another pair of eyes. My personal and professional experience has been that healthy couples seek counseling individually or together, as the circumstances dictate. Just as families have primary care physicians, they should also seek a godly family counselor.

PRACTICES TO PONDER

1. What fruits of the spirit are alive in you? (Galatians 5:22)

2. Is the focus of your marriage child-centered or marital-centered?

3. Are you practicing the thirty minutes a day rule? If not, why?

PRAYER

But the fruit of the Spirit is love, joy, peace, patience, kindness, goodness, faithfulness, gentleness, self-control. (Galatians 5:22–23)

—CHAPTER SIXTEEN—
CHRIST-CENTERED, MARRIAGE-CENTERED, CHILD-CENTERED

The flowchart of an authentic, wisdom-driven family should read "Christ-Centered, Marriage-Centered, Child-Centered." Once children come into the picture, many couples are gradually consumed by child rearing, losing their focus on God and each other. Although our children bring us great joy, none of us are fully prepared for the arrival of our first child. Our sense of love and responsibility are forever changed. In today's world, many couples gradually become overly focused on the lives of their children, neglecting each other and time with the Lord.

CHRIST CENTERED—CHOOSE THE TRUTH

Every truth is God's truth, just as every sin begins with a lie. Love and truth walk together just as their opposites, hate and lies, walk together. From the beginning, when Adam and Eve disobeyed God, believing the lies Satan told them, fear and shame took over instead of love. "There is no fear in love, but perfect love casts out fear. For fear has to do with punishment, and whoever fears has not been perfected in love" (1 John 4:18). Even though Adam and Eve disobeyed God, he still went looking for them. Why? It is all about relationship. God wants us to be his children. You cannot complete yourself with anyone else because our ultimate belonging is with God and his love. Only in our relationship with Jesus will we fulfill our unique passion and purpose.

Christ's love changes everything. As we deeply experience the lavish love and trustworthy forgiveness of Jesus Christ, following his footsteps, our lives bear testimony to his power and grace. Only then are we able to treat others with the same lavish love and trustworthy forgiveness.

WALKING IN LOVE AND TRUST

Trust is essential for love to flourish. We cover up with lies when we have done something wrong, not wanting to deal with the truth. Trying to prove something relentlessly gets in the way of being our authentic selves and experiencing love and trust. The truth is enough in and of itself.

Hiding behind a false self takes the focus off God onto self. The root of all false selves is fear and shame. In the Garden of Eden after Adam and Eve ate the apple disobeying God, they were gripped with fear and shame, hiding from God. Fig leaves became the first false self. We feel fear and shame when we unpack the prideful deception inherent in living a self-centered life. Love and trust come from abiding with God.

PUTTING THE PRINCIPLES OF TRUST INTO PRACTICE

In *Braving the Wilderness: The Quest for True Belonging and the Courage to Stand Alone*, bestselling author Brené Brown identified seven elements of trust useful in trusting ourselves and others.[1]

- Boundaries: Learning to set, hold, and respect boundaries. The challenge is letting go of being liked and the fear of disappointing others.

- Reliability: Learning to say what we mean and mean what we say. The challenge is not overcommitting and overpromising to please others or prove ourselves.
- Accountability: Learning how to step up, be accountable, take responsibility, and issue meaningful apologies when we're wrong. The challenge is letting go of blame and staying out of shame.
- Vault: Learning how to keep confidences, to recognize what's ours to share and what's not. The challenge is to stop using gossip, common enemy intimacy, and oversharing as a way to hotwire connection.
- Integrity: Learning how to practice our values even when it is uncomfortable and hard. [I would add to be honest and trustworthy.] The challenge is choosing courage over comfort in those moments.
- Nonjudgmental: Learning how to give and receive help. The challenge is letting go of helper and fixer as our identity and the source of our self-worth.
- Generosity: Learning how to set the boundaries that allow us to be generous in our assumptions about others. The challenge is being honest and clear with others about what's okay and not okay.

MARRIAGE-CENTERED

The marital relationship is the cornerstone of family dynamics. Without friendship and love, that cornerstone crumbles. In a healthy marriage, both partners experience intimacy as well as individual and spiritual growth. Intimacy grows when couples nurture, appreciate, and confide in one another. Distance grows when couples clam up, blow up, and blame one another. Maintaining a balance between a close, caring relationship with your spouse while retaining autonomy is key. Few master the process.

When I practiced marital therapy, the big issues like addictions or unfaithfulness did not cause marital breakdown. More commonly, the problem was relatively simple conflicts resulting from a lack of knowledge about what the other person needed or what hurt them. A common issue for wives was not feeling cherished or valued. The guys often felt disrespected or were struggling due to a sexual drought. Another common source of breakdown I saw was relationships with the children dominated the marital relationship.

How a husband and a wife relate to one another establishes the emotional climate of the home. Love is a decision that begins with honoring one another. Gentleness and kindness are the currency of love—anger and unforgiveness erode intimacy. Children learn from observing their parents. When parents are affectionate, kids sense love and feel secure. If anger and conflict reign, then children feel anxious and unsettled. What are your children witnessing?

Both the child's security and the quality of the parent-child bonding are largely dependent upon the quality of the marriage. As counter cultural as it may be, this is one of the many reasons I favor marriage over partnering. In marriage, there is a stronger sense of commitment, but also greater involvement of the extended families, providing additional support and resources.

According to Philip Cowan, PhD professor of psychology at the University of California Berkeley, "Children definitely learn how to give and take, how to handle anger, and how to express their feelings by observing their parents' model of relating. New research indicates that the way children get along with other kids, including their siblings, closely correlates with how their parents get along with each other."[2]

RELATIONSHIP PATTERNS AND KIDS

From an early age, children are acutely aware of the emotional tone of their parents' interactions. Children are particularly distressed when parents appear unable to resolve their differences. One study suggested that children as young as two years old feel better about an argument when they know it is settled. Children witness successful conflict resolution if a couple argues and then solves the dispute amicably. Children learn how to resolve their disputes with negotiation and compromise rather than aggression or temper tantrums.

On numerous occasions, I have witnessed tension or conflict between parents impacting the child. On one such occasion, a blonde, pink-bowed toddler accompanied her parents to my office. They had come concerning behavior problems involving her fifth-grade brother. During the conference, she happily played in the corner with a doll. Suddenly, her parents were drawn into a heated discussion regarding the discipline of their son. Immediately, the little girl stopped playing and went to her parents. She stood between them holding each of them by the hand becoming a human conduit, connecting her parents.

From the time children are born until they leave the home, they learn how relationships work at the parents' knees. They see their parents laughing, arguing, sharing, conferring, crying, comforting, yelling, hugging, and hopefully praying. These multitude of images are internalized, forming a template for the child's view of how Mom and Dad treat each other, how parents and children communicate, and how siblings interact.

Children from loving families get a bird's eye view of what healthy relations look like. They learn trust, lasting friendship, and love. Their home feels secure and safe.

As previously mentioned, there is a close link between the marital bond and the parent-child relationship. When marriage works well, children are nourished and rewarded by their parents' love and appreciation for each other, and are supported by their cooperation.

Children have a deep and long-lasting desire for their parents to live together in love and harmony. Conversely, children have a deep fear of their parents fighting and ultimately going their separate ways. This becomes a testimony to the child that love is conditional—if Mom and Dad stop loving each other, they can stop loving me. This deals a major blow to the wellbeing of the child, paying the price for their parents' inability to love one another.

BLURRED BOUNDARIES

Becky and her husband Sam had said goodbye to their youngest son, James, as he began his freshman year at a Big Ten university in the Midwest. On the return flight home, Becky became increasingly aware of how distant she and Sam had become. She wondered how it happened and if they would be heading toward a divorce. Theirs was a child-centered family—both Becky and Sam were involved in their son's sports and musical activities, attending all the games and performances. Gradually, Becky began making family decisions—guiding and directing the boys without consulting her husband. With their nest empty, Becky noticed more acutely the distance and disconnect that had grown between Sam and herself. Becky was worried and concerned but determined to repair and restore the relationship. Rather than take a promotion at work involving extensive traveling, Becky focused all her attention on Sam for the first time in twenty plus years in a courageous and hopeful effort to save and restore their marriage to its rightful place.

Becky and Sam did the hard work of introspection, embracing the painful truth of where they were in their relationship, to address each long-standing issue one at a time. With the help of God, and through the help of a trusted counselor, they were able to move forward and prioritize their relationship to the place where it should have been all along.

When the priorities of the couple flow from God-centered to marriage-centered to child-centered, the family is properly balanced. Trouble occurs when the position of the child becomes exalted and personal boundaries are blurred. When there is distance in the marriage, often one of the children is drawn into an overly close position with a parent—usually the mom—to fill the gap. This has serious ramifications for all concerned, frequently alienating the child from siblings and peers due to over identification with an adult, as well as a sense of entitlement. When a mother becomes best friends with her daughter, this indicates the boundaries are blurred—the mother meeting her own needs through the daughter.

While working in schools, I came across many women with prestigious careers who, following the birth of their first or second child, decided to modify or give up their careers to concentrate on raising their kids. The same vim and vigor they brought to their careers was focused on child rearing. At times, this focus was so intense both the husband and children suffered.

Practices to Ponder

1. Are you and your spouse speaking in one voice and on the same team?
2. Are the boundaries between you and your kids firmly established?
3. Are you accountable for your own behavior and actions?

Prayer

Teach me your way, O Lord, that I may walk in your truth; unite my heart to fear your name. I give thanks to you, O Lord my God, with my whole heart, and I will glorify your name forever. (Psalm 86:11–12)

—CHAPTER SEVENTEEN—
ABIDING

Whoever you are, no matter how lonely,
the world offers itself to your imagination ...
announcing your place
in the family of things.
—from "Wild Geese" by Mary Oliver[1]

A COLLECTIVE VOICE LIFTED HIGH

To abide means to remain, dwell, continue, or endure. Jesus says to let his words abide in us (John 15:7). Incorporating God's Word into our minds and hearts is how we dwell with him and learn to know him intimately. Scripture adjusts our focus from earthly priorities to heavenly ones and aligns our thoughts with God's, so we know how to pray according to his will instead of ours.

Obedience is an essential aspect of abiding. As we read and meditate upon God's Word, it convicts us of sin so we can repent and be cleansed. As we devour his Word, the desire to obey his Word grows until there is no other option. When you abide and obey, love is a byproduct—love and obedience walk hand in hand. As Jesus said, "Whoever has my commandments and keeps them, he it is who loves me. And he who loves me will be loved by my Father, and I will love him and manifest myself to him" (John 4:21).

I (Jess) woke up early one August morning, a couple of months after our family of four moved to St. Louis, Missouri, so my husband, Andy, could attend a pastoral graduate program at Concordia Seminary. Rain poured down outside our brick flat, and I was exhausted from staying up throughout the night nursing my eight-month-old son, Rocky, who was teething. My three-year-old would be up soon, starting a day fulfilling endless to-dos and toddler requests. I grabbed my Bible and headed through the rain to the coffee shop while the kids and Andy were still asleep.

I had been reading the previous day from Genesis 16, and God spoke to me through his Word about his promises and waiting. I was eager to continue with my reading of Genesis 16. I found God speaking to me in that shared space of waiting and frustration where Sarai and I both found ourselves: God made a clear promise, yet years went by. Struck by Abram and Sarai's struggle of waiting and taking matters into their own hands, I resonated with their weariness in waiting. They were fed up even though God had promised to answer them in his time. Their experience struck me in a new way, as there were a couple of areas in my life about which I believed God's promises but was growing weary waiting. "God, I need encouragement today. Please encourage me," I prayed.

The downpour seemed to bring a freshness, a cleansing. I sprinted to my car, already soaked, and drove a short distance through the downpour, craving the Word which I knew would befriend me.

At the coffee shop, I sat sipping my drip Kaldi's coffee. Warm behind the window, I glanced toward a group of five twenty-something-year-old guys a couple of tables away—clean cut, polo shirts, and eagerly engaged with each other. Wow, these guys were up and at 'em, dressed and connecting before seven on a weekday morning. They were leaning in, actively listening to each person talking, making eye contact, and exchanging stories with what seemed like genuine love and joy between them.

I paused from my reading and picked up some of their discussion. They were referencing the seminary and hermeneutics, and an article that concerned them. One of them wanted prayer for writing a purposeful and loving response. The others took note with seriousness. Another asked for prayer for a good start to the semester. These young men were seminarians like my husband but much younger, as my husband's program was for second-career church workers. After exchanging what was on each of their hearts and acknowledging each other's hurts, joys, and concerns, they began to pray and ended by together lifting their voices in The Lord's Prayer.

> Our Father in heaven, hallowed be your name. Your kingdom come, your will be done, on earth as it is in heaven. Give us this day our daily bread, and forgive us our debts, as we also have forgiven our debtors. And lead us not into temptation, but deliver us from evil. (Matthew 6:9–13)

I was encouraged by these young men in Christ, so connected with themselves and God and each other—men who clearly walked with and loved the Lord. I felt emboldened by their voices lifted high, as they gave the Lord their day, their sins, and their trust. They were unabashed and on display for all to see, not in a showy way, but just genuinely, tucked into the back of a small coffee shop one quiet and raining Missouri early morning.

God more than answered my prayer for encouragement. He held me up in his truth, spoken and washed over me by the voices of these men strong in the Lord. Always, if we are open and expectant, God's grace and washing are available to us. That morning, the sound and fragrance of the Lord was sweet. I was lifted up. My quiet time was made loud by these faithful men in the best way. I was reminded of the truth and timelessness of God's promise to deliver and strengthen me. The timeless truth of Scripture was reinforced by these brothers in Christ, who were living authentically before themselves, each other, and their creator, in maturity.

I felt cleansed from the need to take matters into my own hands regarding the future or questions unanswered, reminded simply to wait, to trust, and to be encouraged. Living life authentically involves struggle and looks weird to a world that lives contrary to Christ-connectedness. This life involves the death and mourning of old ways of doing and being so new insights can be ushered in and grow.

He is faithful to lift us up in due time and to allow us to be fruitful, to deliver answers to longstanding questions when he decides the time is right. Do not lose hope or lose sight if, when you decide to dive in, you notice changes stirring up a struggle within. In my experience, the storm is often part of the cleansing process, leveling that which needs to go, watering that which is to come.

Three years later, I returned to this section of the book I had written shortly after that day. I see now it took three years for God to answer many of the questions I pressed him for that particular day. For three years, I prayed many of the same prayers and lived in that space of hope in suffering. I now see the answers and fruit of the soil tilled and planted then as I waited for growth, then life, then fruit. I understand now in a greater way the plight of Sarah, who God changed and blessed despite her misunderstandings of God's plans, despite her impatience, despite her own will coming against the Lord's. I understand better now that God has a promise to fulfill for each of us, and just as Abraham and Sarah waited their entire lives for God's plan to come to fruition, we also often don't know the ways God works, but we can trust in his goodness, his timing, his purpose in suffering. We can trust that his mercies are new every morning, and that great is his faithfulness (Lamentations 3:22–23).

ALIGNMENT WITH GOD'S TRUTH

Oswald Chambers, author of the most enduring devotional of all time and one that I (Jean) have been praying for the past thirty years, *My Utmost for His Highest*, made a profound statement concerning the purpose of prayer— "Prayer is perfect and complete oneness with God."[2]

SILENCE AND SOLITUDE

Dallas Willard called silence and solitude the 'two most radical disciplines of the Christian life'. Solitude is the practice of being absent from people and things to attend to God. Silence is the practice of quieting every inner and outer voice to attend to God. Henri Nouwen said that 'without solitude it is almost impossible to live a spiritual life.[3]

This time of silence and solitude does not just happen but must be deliberated and defined. For me the time is outside in my backyard early in the morning when birds are cooing, and the neighborhood is asleep.

One of the things I (Jean) like best about this last stage of my life is the silence and solitude of being alone. I was alone for the first time in my adult life after becoming widowed—I wasn't married, my sons were grown, and I wasn't working. I realized the beauty and peace of silence and solitude. There is a special strength that is born in solitude. Strength is found not in busyness and noise, but in quietness.

RESTORATION

Early every morning, I toss a sweatshirt over my PJs with latte, Bible, and devotionals in hand, and I head to my backyard to pray. Beginning the day in the quiet of the morning outside connects me to God not only through prayer but also through the power of his creation, the nature all around me. There is something about being outside that reminds me of the peace of our loving God.

Being outside brings your soul closer to God which is restorative. You pause to absorb the beauty of the fluffy clouds and bright blue skies. Joyfully, I watch the hawks gliding on air currents. Looks like fun. In the twenty-third Psalm, David wrote how God took him outside to give him rest and comfort. "The LORD is my shepherd; I shall not want. He makes me lie down in green pastures. He leads me beside still waters. He restores my soul. He leads me in paths of righteousness for his name's sake" (Psalm 23:1–3).

I settle in to spend time with my dear Lord and Savior. I find a peace and joy I have never known while watching the clouds float over the Saddleback Mountains, looking down at the houses in the valley below, listening for the gentle voice of Jesus. I savor being alone in the presence of Jesus.

THE GENTLE WHISPER

God said, "Be still, and know that I am God" (Psalm 46:10). As I listen, spending unhurried time in prayer and meditation, I begin to hear the "gentle whisper" in the depths of my heart and soul. In Scripture, Jesus refers to his relationship with his children as a shepherd who gathers and protects his sheep. "My sheep hear my voice, and I know them, and they follow me" (John 10:27).

In the devotional, *Streams in the Desert*, this phenomenon is described beautifully when A. B. Simpson, a Canadian minister, author, and founder of Christian and Missionary Alliance, is quoted.

> The 'gentle whisper' became for me the voice of prayer, wisdom, and service. No longer did I need to work so hard to think, pray, or trust because the Holy Spirit's 'gentle whisper' in my heart was God's prayer in the secret places in my soul. It was His answer to all my questions, and His life and strength for my soul and body. His voice became the essence of all knowledge, prayer, and blessings, for it was the living God himself as my life and my all.[4]

THE VINE AND THE BRANCHES

While reading the Bible one day, I came upon the familiar story of the vine and the branches. Jesus said, "I am the true vine, and my Father is the vinedresser" (John 15:1). "Abide in me, and I in you. As the branch cannot bear fruit by itself, unless it abides in the vine, neither can you, unless you abide in me" (John 15:4). Just as when the branch is grafted into the vine and the sap from the vine flows through the branch, when one abides in Jesus, the crucified one, his power flows through us. In this process, we too experience our Gethsemane putting to death the old sinful self and being transformed by abiding with our Holy Lord. God is all about making us holy.

This of course requires one to give up self-independence and determination. You will find it hard to receive the power of Jesus if you, as the branch, keep running off and doing your own thing. Staying connected to the vine is not optional if you want to walk in his light.

According to John Eldredge, "The secret of Christianity is not self-transformation but the life of Christ in you—allowing his life to become your life. His revolution is not self-transformation but his transformation in you from the inside out as you receive his life and allow him to live through you. Vine branch. Anything else is madness."[5]

The loving presence of Jesus is within your heart all day long, saying he's there for you, guiding you with his right hand. He will never leave you. He is your loving Savior who died to redeem you. Right now, as you are.

Oswald Chambers writes: "The wonders of conviction of sin, forgiveness, and holiness are so interwoven that it is only the forgiven person who is truly holy. He proves he is forgiven by being the opposite of what he was previously, by the grace of God. Repentance always brings a person to the point of saying I have sinned."[6]

Andrew Murray wrote the following in the classic, *Abide in Christ*.

> O Jesus, our crucified Redeemer, teach us not only to believe on thee, but to abide in Thee, to take Thy cross not only as the ground of our pardon, but also as the law of our life. O teach us to love it not only because on it Thou does bear our curse, but because on it we enter into the closest fellowship with Thyself, and our crucified with Thee. And teach us, that as we yield ourselves wholly to be possessed of the Spirit in which Thou didst bear the cross, we shall be partakers of the power and blessing to which the cross alone gives access.[7]

PRACTICES TO PONDER

1. Does God's Word remain, dwell, and continue in me?

2. Am I more preoccupied with talking to God in prayer than listening to what he said in his Word?

3. What are some idols or unhealthy attachments God wants me to address today?

4. Have you ever experienced a painful circumstance that, in the long run, turned out to be a blessing?

5. What are some idols or unhealthy attachments God wants you to address today?

PRAYER

For thus said the LORD GOD, the Holy One of Israel, "In returning and rest you shall be saved; in quietness and in trust shall be your strength." (Isaiah 30:15)

Blessed are the people who know the festal shout, who walk, O LORD, in the light of your face, who exult in your name all the day and in your righteousness are exalted. (Psalm 89:15–16)

—CHAPTER EIGHTEEN—
THE COMPASSIONATE "WE"

I know, you never intended to be in this world.
But you're in it all the same.
so why not get started immediately ...
I am speaking from the fortunate platform
of many years,
none of which, I think, I ever wasted.
—Mary Oliver, "The Fourth Sign of the Zodiac," Part 3[1]

AUTHENTIC BEING

Authentic: From the Greek *authentikos*, warranted, from autos, self, and entea, instruments, tools.

1. having a genuine original or authority, in opposition to that which is false, fictitious, or counterfeit; being what it purports to be; genuine; true
2. of approved authority; trustworthy; reliable[2]

Upon the completion of the initial draft of this book, and after we had submitted two lengthy proposals and were awaiting news of interest from a potential publisher, I (Jess) went to the gorgeous St. Louis Basilica for solitude, to be with God in a space dedicated to quiet and prayer. Opening one of the large carved wooden doors, I entered the foyer, my eyes instantly drawn up to the gold, glass, and stonework of the mosaiced ceiling. I love that art in designated places of prayer often draws the eye up to heaven.

Ground was broken to begin building the St. Louis Basilica in 1907, to be dedicated to St. Louis, based upon plans that began in 1871. The structure itself was completed in 1914 and the mosaic installation in 1988.

It was as if God was saying to me,

> You and Jean, whose respective lives will span a length of time greater than you will on your own, will create something together, as Saints in the faith, who link time. What you have started here will carry into the future, just as this stone building withstands, though its plans began in 1871. What you have started will be something that others can stand on in faith, a place to go for peace where people will find rest for their souls and to refuel their faith in Jesus and be encouraged to find beauty and joy. You, individually and together, as members of the body of Christ, are basilicas, standing boldly, proclaiming beauty and truth in a world that desperately needs such places. You will proclaim truth—truth of Scripture, which is the basis of love, so people can, in finding truth, find themselves—find yourselves, in me.

Above me was the embossed face of St. Paul, composed of thousands of fragments of glass, stone, and marble. I thought of Paul's life—his struggle, his anguish, his transformation, and God's mighty use of his life. Paul lived out his later days in complete authenticity—dedicated to his purpose and passion unto his death. The fragments reminded me of how we are all fragmented, but, in Christ, become whole. All the many disjointed pieces of our identity and personhood, light and dark, begin to make sense in the context of our worthiness as God's beloved—forgiven and loved.

Surrounding this broken yet whole image of Paul, hovering over me like a golden shining umbrella, were the words from 2 Timothy 4:7, "I have fought the good fight, I have finished the race, I have kept the faith." I immediately thought of Jean, writing as an older woman, who echoes these words of Paul, "I have fought the good fight, I have finished the race, I have kept the faith."

In the book of Second Timothy, Paul, now an old man writing his last known letter, refers to Timothy as "my dear son" though they were not actually father and son. Paul took Timothy under his wing as a mentor which turned into a love like father and son. We notice Paul's care and concern for Timothy when he writes what he knows to him regarding life, faith, and truth. Paul says he thanks God as he constantly remembers Timothy in his prayers (2 Timothy 1:3), that he longs to see Timothy (v. 4), and that he is reminded of his sincere faith (v. 5). He goes on to say he is writing to remind Timothy to "fan into flame the gift of God, which is in you through the laying on of my hands (v. 6)."

Paul imparted the life-giving traditional Jewish blessing honoring his mentee with words of life and worth. After reminding Timothy of the blessing he has given, he says, "For God gave us a spirit not of fear but of power and love and self-control." He reminds Timothy not to be discouraged by suffering, but that, even though imprisoned because of the Gospel, the grace of Christ Jesus "who abolished death and brought life and immortality to light through the gospel" (vv. 7–10).

God has consistently raised leaders up to guide and mentor others in the faith. This is integral to fulfilling our potential and calling—having someone be the skin and bones of God's love toward us. Someone who can remind us of our worth and value and be there out of choice and commitment and genuine concern. The obligation of familial connection removed, mentors of the faith often provide the gift of love and guidance in addition to family and friends that fulfills a place of wisdom and kinship in a unique way. In the case of Jean and me, we have mutually benefited from our God-gifted connection. In one season, we may be a mentee while in another season, we may be a mentor.

Finding Oneself, Finding God

The process of finding our true self is intrinsically interwoven with our growing relationship with God, from whom we find our origin and authority as well as the courage to oppose that which is false. Through our experiences of suffering and betrayal, we turn to God and begin the process of becoming who we are meant to be, our authentic truest self. Only as we wise women peel off the false masks hiding our real self, do we become available to know and be known by others.

Sue Monk Kidd, author of *When the Heart Waits* wrote,

> The Christ-life doesn't divorce us from our humanity: it causes us to embrace it. It makes us human. It humbles us. Genuine transformation always connects us to our essential nature, both the sacred and profane. When we go through its passages, we plumb the depths of our humanity. We become intimate with what lies inside—the wild and untamed, the orphaned and abused, the soiled and unredeemed. We hold our falseness in our hands and trace our fingers over the masks we wear, like blind people feeling the unseen faces of those she wants to know. We stare into the sockets of pain and glimpse the naked truth of who we are.[3]

We cannot be authentic without realizing who we are in our humanity, who we are in Christ, and the redemption that has been made to bridge the gap. We live in authenticity when we are honest about all parts of ourselves, accepting them as Christ does. Only in understanding Christ's love for us can we extend that same love and empathy to ourselves and others. French paleontologist and theologian Pierre Teilhard de Chardin said, "To be united, that is to become the other, while remaining oneself."[4] It is only when we come to grips with the truth about ourselves, shedding all pretense and hypocrisy, surrendering to Jesus, that we cross over to genuine oneness in understanding the link of our common humanity with others while maintaining our authentic self.

Fear of the Lord is the foundation of spiritual wisdom and knowledge. Fear consists of awe, adoration, and submission to the will of God. When you submit to Jesus you exchange your attitudes and goals for his. "The LORD takes pleasure in those who fear him, in those who hope in his steadfast love" (Psalm 147:11).

In the process of sanctification, which is being made holy through the power of God, our purpose becomes God's purpose. The process of sanctification begins in this life and is made complete upon our union with God in heaven. At first, we don't realize this truth, but as long as we follow our own desires, agendas, and ambitions we cannot be completely aligned with God's interests.

Charles F. Stanley of In Touch Ministries writes,

> The heavenly Father desires to have an intimate relationship with each of his children. We get to enjoy this closeness by engaging with Him in His Word and in prayer. Intimacy comes from a deepening fellowship that leads to our greater understanding of God, His Word, and His will for our life. As we spend time with Him and obey Him, He begins to conform us to His image. Then He works through us, and we reflect Him to those around us, like a light set on a lampstand. (Matthew 5:14–16)[5]

LIVING YOUR IDENTITY

Remembering Jesus loves you, that you are his beloved, provides a rock-solid foundation for your life. With your identity securely anchored in Jesus, you can bring his truth and transparency into relations with others. Colossians says, "Put on then, as God's chosen ones, holy and beloved, compassionate hearts, kindness, humility, meekness, and patience … And above all these put on love, which binds everything together in perfect harmony" (3:12,14).

Only as we contemplate God's Word and become one with him in prayer do we encounter the life of God, and our soul gradually becomes more like Jesus as we are filled with his holiness, his love, and his compassion. Oswald Chambers writes,

> The true expression of Christian character is not in good-doing but in God-likeness. If the spirit of God has transformed you within, you will exhibit divine characteristics in your life, not just good human characteristics. God's life in us expresses itself as God's life, not as human life trying to be godly. The secret of a Christian's life is that the supernatural becomes natural in him as a result of the grace of God, and the experiences of this become evident in the practical everyday details of life, not in times of intimate fellowship with God. And when we come in contact with things that create confusion and a flurry of activity, we find to our own amazement that we have the power to stay wonderfully poised even in the center of it all.[6]

Mature Christians realize the goal of life is not about escaping to Hawaii, taking as many cruises as possible, or being the richest person on the planet. The goal of human existence is total complete union with Jesus Christ. "And this is his commandment, that we believe in the name of his Son Jesus Christ and love one another, just as he has commanded us. Whoever keeps his commandments abides in God, and God in him. And by this we know that he abides in us, by the Spirit whom he has given us" (1 John 3:23–24). Without God's grace we can never move beyond anger and offer forgiveness, can never really love. We seek the daily process of being saved, delivered, healed, and surrendered to Jesus.

Therefore, I focus not on me, but how I practice the presence of God when engaging with others—how I serve God by treating others with love, empathy, and compassion. Not just the others I like and relate to with heightened empathy but simply, all others—the poor, sick, hungry—all humanity. This is the "compassionate we."

THE COMPASSIONATE "WE"

Jesus's call on our lives means deliberately identifying ourselves with God's interest in other people.

Sue Monk Kidd author of *When the Heart Waits* wrote: "As the True Self is born within us, the initial movement of soul is from the collective 'they' to the ground of an authentic 'I.' That's holy ground, yet God calls us to a ground even holier: God calls us from the authentic 'I' toward a compassionate 'we.'"[7]

What does the compassionate we look like? The definition of "compassion" is clear. Compassion means sorrow for the sufferings of another, while empathy is defined by the Bible as the deep feeling of concern for suffering and needy people. These characteristics are the very nature of God.

God wants us to comfort others with the comfort we have received from him. As the Bible states: "Blessed be the God and Father of our LORD Jesus Christ, the Father of mercies and God of all comfort, who comforts us in all our affliction, so that we may be able to comfort those who are in any affliction, with the comfort with which we ourselves are comforted by God" (2 Corinthians 1:3–4).

I realized I gradually grew in maturity and wisdom when I took my heartbreak to God, seeking his help. Suffering can build your character and prepare you to help others who are struggling. While going through a drama such as divorce, only after you process the pain and find God's healing will you be equipped to help others. Your maturity and wisdom grow when you draw closer to Jesus during tough times, tapping into his power. Enduring adversity equips you to comfort others, your empathy for others spilling over into their lives.

You will find, as I have found over the years, you're most effective at comforting those who are enduring trials you have already experienced. To quote the Greek playwright, Aeschylus, "He who learns must suffer. And even in our sleep, pain, which we cannot forget, falls drop by drop upon the heart, until, in our despair, against our will, comes wisdom through the awful grace of God."[8]

CONNECTED THROUGH STORY

How do we get to know each other? By listening to each other's stories. Everyone has a story. Listening provides perspective into their pain and what has shaped them, and with listening come understanding and grace. It is difficult not to like someone once you understand their past.

I (Jean) learned this well while working as a guidance counselor in Highland Park High School. I scheduled an appointment with parents feeling disgruntled over their inability to provide adequately for their child's needs. Upon listening to the parent, hearing their pain, experiences, and what had shaped them, I often realized they provided much better care than they had received. New understanding, insight, and empathy sprung up in me, laying a foundation for us to work together to invoke change.

In an interview between Michelle Obama and Tracee Ellis Ross, the pair discussed building bridges through storytelling. Ms. Ross, the daughter of singer Diana Ross, is best known for her role in the sitcom "Blackish" for which she won a Golden Globe Award in 2017. Ms. Ross commented, "Knowing other people's stories is how we connect with them. That's where the compassion is ignited. If people who don't know you hate you because of some idea they've made up about you, your honest life story is the thing that dismantles the walls between us."[9]

We were not meant to walk alone. We are sociable beings. As you pursue friendship you will want to know their story. Remember they will have a false self just as you did, constructed to avoid rejection and to win approval. Encourage their true self to find a voice and come alive while not getting tripped up by what their false self has to offer. Recently I attended a funeral where one of the songs was "I Did It My Way" by Frank Sinatra. I thought, "My way is the wrong way."

EMPATHY

Caring and empathy connect us to other human beings. In seeing things from someone else's perspective, we live outside of ourselves, and walk in someone else's shoes. As Atticus tells Scout in *To Kill a Mockingbird*, "You never really understand a person until you consider things from another's point of view—until you climb into his skin and walk around in it."[10]

Jesus is full of compassion. When John the Baptist needed confirmation concerning Jesus, he sent this message: "The blind receive their sight, the lame walk, lepers are cleansed, and the deaf hear, the dead are raised up, the poor have good news preached to them" (Luke 7:22).

"Caring is what deepens and grows your very soul and builds your moral code," explains Martin L. Hoffman, a psychologist and professor emeritus of clinical and developmental psychology at New York University. "It's the soil in which integrity grows and every other virtue."[11]

That may be why God made empathy the first moral emotion to develop in children. Around two years of age, toddlers begin recognizing the feelings of others, in particular pain. We've all seen a toddler try to comfort an upset sibling or playmate. Developmental psychologists have documented infants displaying sympathetic distress. For example, a child even as young as one year will pull his or her mother across a room to comfort a crying infant. I have a fond memory of my son Tom hiking with his daughter, Haley, then about twelve months old on his back. Sitting on a rock, resting for a moment, she laughingly offered him a drink from her bottle.

While children will naturally begin to display empathy, they need you to guide the process. To foster empathetic behavior such as sharing, helping, and comforting others, guide them toward understanding the inner world of feelings—their own and others. This is done effectively when we teach our children to look ahead at their own behavior. What is the impact of your behavior on yourself and on others? This is authoritative discipline in a nutshell. Diana Baumrind defined the power of practices that nurture the development of empathy, of altruism, of conscience, and of moral reasoning as authoritative parenting. When parents offer an appropriate balance of demands and nurturance, they maximize the possibility of their children growing up with the following characteristics:[12]

1. The drive to work toward goals that are both personally and socially desirable.

2. The courage to persevere when faced with obstacles.

3. The ability to control impulses.

4. The ability to be accountable to themselves and others.

5. An understanding of what is right and wrong.

6. A tendency to choose right over wrong.

If you were not raised this way, begin to think through each of these points and find accountability for each area where you would like to see growth and healing in your life. It is important to work through these areas that have never matured to be able to guide our children. If you were raised this way, you can thank your parents for giving you a solid footing when others might have to work to gain such footing.

We can only give out what we have been given and modeled, and thankfully, God guides with grace and dignity, kindness and compassion. He always gives fresh starts, and his mercies are new every morning (Lamentations 3:22–23 paraphrased). No matter where we are in this process—of life, growth, parenting, singleness, married, widowed, divorced—he is there to forgive us in our failures, celebrate and clap for us in our triumphs, and direct us with his shepherd's staff, gently leading us forward, never backward, but always pointing us in the right direction. He allows us to be, yet gently guides if we are willing.

PRACTICES TO PONDER

1. What would your answer be if God asks you how you loved those people he brought to you?

2. What could you change in your schedule to allow more time for relationships?

3. Do you thoughts and actions reflect the mind of Jesus?

PRAYER

"Love the LORD your God with all your heart and with all your soul and with all your mind. This is the great and first commandment. And a second is like it: You shall love your neighbor as yourself" (Matthew 22:37–39).

—CHAPTER NINETEEN—
OUT FROM UNDER THE TREE

And the LORD God made for Adam and for his wife
garments of skins and clothed them. (Genesis 3:21)

God invites us to come out from under the tree of hiding
and consistently face the truth. Going awry, we face the
great temptation to look outside of ourselves and hide
from the truth, pretending it is not there. We further hide
when we still feel the same after our quick attempt to
cover it, perhaps with alcohol, or shopping (a personal
favorite of both Jess and Jean), or with sex or academia,
with money, or by tuning out. We hide behind so many
things. God asks us to choose to come out of this hiding.
To sit in that contentious place where we are exposed and
uncomfortable, faced with the truth and any pain that
accompanies it before God, ourselves, and each other.

We can hear, see, and accept a great covering only if we
are willing to come out and be seen in that place of truth.
We find that in some way, the death lost in exposure can
be purposeful and the lesson can give us life and warmth,
just as the animal skin coverings did for Adam and Eve.
The knowledge of the deaths which took place because of
what we have done, what we all have done, can provide a
common ground for community. We see each other's animal

skins and know: "You too?" "And still, love!" We can rest in the assurance we are known, so known, all of us, and so loved. This type of animal-skin, God-covering-us love provides the model for how we are to love, and forgive, and comfort, and speak truth into, and embrace, each other.

We begin to understand the depths of a God who loves us fully anyway, that our friends love us anyway, and that we can, if we dare, love ourselves anyway. What was once burning inside of us, causing us to run and hide and tremble, no longer controls us. In such clarity and such light, we begin to see our story and hold it as a reminder and offering, a connecting point to help another along.

No one is exempt from this process, however wonderful or grievous our pasts. It is the simple truth of the nature of humanity and the nature of sin and death. I believe this is one reason God cautions about making one sin greater than another—because all sin is great and all sin kills little parts of ourselves however "small" the sin is.

We appreciate our healing when we see another hurting in ways we once did and, instead of turning our face, acting as if we have not been there, or hiding, we offer to take their hand as a dear friend. Holding our same hurt as a treasure, we offer it and say, "Me too. Utilize this for life, for growth. I've been there. This is my story." Our hurt transforms into a vehicle of compassion by offering it to others. Just as God offers us such compassion in a collection of stories, we too can take part in the mystery of this great story—this great love.

When we commit to understanding the truth and healing, we accept a call to adventure and embark on our own hero's journey of discovering what has been lost. We may ultimately find ourselves found again through facing various crises of the soul, discovering, and addressing its many wounded places, through examination, and through

God's divine intervention. In repeating this cycle, we can grasp many boons of truth which grant us wisdom, perspective, and godly maturity to better the world together as one body of saints.

SPACE, STORY, AND SACRIFICE

I (Jess) recently read an observation from Sue Monk Kidd's book *Firstlight* that struck me. It is that "the words now, here, and nowhere have the same arrangement of letters, but differ when a small space is inserted. Likewise, a fine space separates us from experiencing our life as nowhere or now here."[1] Her words got me thinking about how often we deny ourselves and others that space. Space to be, to grow and process, space to feel and be held. Allowing ourselves and others to occupy space—to hear another's story, to claim our story. To pause. To reflect. I would argue that such space makes all the difference between awareness or a life of perpetual delirium, between penning our story or letting others write it, between living as casual spectators or key figures. The choice between staying or getting unstuck.

In parenting my young daughter and son, I practice giving them and myself this type of space to be authentic and to be held in that space. Recently, on a car ride home, I became aware of the importance of holding this space and putting it into practice. My daughter was recalling our home we sold in California five months prior—one we had loved but outgrown. We reminisced about our chickens and the flowers we loved. "Will we ever move back to that house?" she asked, hopefully. I looked into her glassy, three-year-old eyes, and held her hand, trying to meet her where she was as she searched me for a pleasing answer. "No," I said, as kindly as I could muster a 'no.' "We won't." Tears began flowing down her plump, baby soft cheeks. She said, "I miss that house." And through more tears, "I can hardly remember what it looks like now."

I gave myself a short moment to pause and gather, giving myself space before I could offer it to her. I was tempted to jump in with a lot of reassurance and happy talk about visiting and going back, but I knew in that moment of pause such a response would come at the expense of not seeing her in her pain and allowing her to feel and be seen. A cheer-up speech would come at the expense of not acknowledging her feelings at this moment, moving forward without being here fully. God gives us time. He does not ask us to ignore our feelings or pretend to be and feel something we are not. I have grown enough in his wisdom to try to mimic that love—the only way I can help my daughter to grow whole.

We sat there in the car, I in the front passenger seat, and my daughter in her car seat behind the driver's, hands held. She cried, and I simply held her hand saying, "It is sad. We miss that house. I miss it too." And miraculously, as being truly seen always does, the couple of minutes of full and necessary mourning subsided like a winter leaf upon solid wet ground laid still, bare, and held.

I could see her gather herself, her spirit lifted. Her tone changed, the tears dried up and she asked, "Mom, can I have a sip of your drink?" I passed my drink back to her, and we carried on with the drive home. I could feel the illumination of sun shining in on us—warmth, love, and hope could be born again.

In that moment, I knew the Spirit was teaching me a lesson about being seen and about space. I also felt sadness for all the times I'd missed it in parenting her so far—realizing this lesson in giving space has taken me so long to learn. I hadn't handled it well many times before when my own frustrations took up the space that needed to be available to see her. I was also reminded of the importance of grace.

The word grace means "gift." To give grace, or a gift, always involves a sacrifice, especially concerning the biblical connotation of grace. Giving grace is offering up our sacrifice, and sometimes that sacrifice involves understanding the thousand times we've handled something wrong, or not been courageous enough to really know and see, to then arrive at what we should have been doing all along. Grace is offering this gift of awareness of the sacrifice to others and ourselves.

I want to live out of this place of seeing the truth and offer it to others. I want to have the bravery and courage to continue feeling and allow others the space to feel and heal. Giving grace to ourselves means continually reminding ourselves, "I was there, but now I am here," and living here.

PRACTICES TO PONDER

1. Am I taking the time to slow down and spend time with Jesus?

2. Instead of pretending, do I desire the truth in my innermost being?

3. Am I seeking the help of others to reach into deep issues in my heart and open the door to healing?

4. Do I hold grudges or am I quick to forgive?

5. Am I taking the time to listen to my child's heart?

PRAYER

Dear Jesus, search me and know me. Come into the deep places of my heart that have been misunderstood and wounded. Come and be my counselor and bring others into my life for support as well.

—CHAPTER TWENTY—
FROM WISDOM, FOR ALWAYS

Tell me, what is it you plan to do
with your one wild and precious life?
—"The Summer Day" by Mary Oliver[1]

A LIFE OF LEGACY

As one grows older, there is a tendency to look back over your life to see how far you have come. The first half of my (Jean's) life, God was in my life—the second half, I was in God's life. Without a relationship with Jesus Christ, there is little faith and no power. God gives you wisdom when you trust and obey him. "Hear, my son, and accept my words, that the years of your life may be many. I have taught you the way of wisdom; I have led you in the paths of uprightness. When you walk, your step will not be hampered, and if you run, you will not stumble" (Proverbs 4:10–12).

There is a ripple effect when you choose to be compassionate. Making that choice impacts how you interact with God, and extends to the family and friends around you. Such is my experience, by extending compassion and forgiveness to GK, the rest of my life became a testimony to Jesus. These characteristics are integral to who Jesus is and who we are in Jesus. The book of Colossians reminds us to, "Put on then, as God's chosen ones, holy and beloved, compassionate hearts, kindness, humility, meekness, and patience, bearing with one another and, if one has a complaint against another, forgiving each other; as the Lord has forgiven you, so you also must forgive. And above all these put on love, which binds everything together in perfect harmony" (3:12–14). As love flows throughout the family, harmony is restored in all relationships.

Your true authentic identity is in God, you are his masterpiece, created to follow his purpose. God established your identity and purpose before you were born. Your purpose is connected to the desires of your heart. You become a member of God's household, a child of God, when you accept Jesus as your Lord and Savior. You are his masterpiece filled with grace. The closer you get to Jesus, walking in harmony with his spirit, the more your true inner self shines forth.

Following GK's death, I dedicated the last stage of my life to Jesus.

Thus began an exciting adventure, living life following Jesus. Waiting each day for the blessings and surprises Jesus has in store. The spiritual insight of Jesus steers us away from danger and disaster, helping us speak and live in balance, kindness, and love. Dropping any masquerade, you can authentically follow Jesus Christ in all areas of your life by the power of the Holy Spirit. I became alive with the energy of Jesus through the power of the Holy Spirit. The fragrances of the Holy Spirit flow out of me to others. It is contagious. "Blessed are the pure in heart, for they shall see God" (Matthew 5:8).

PROTECTING YOUR TRUE IDENTITY

The burden of the false self is that it requires constant maintenance. If your false self is money, you will always need more. If your false self is performance, you will earn another degree, score another goal, or be driven to climb the career ladder. If you are a people-pleaser, there will always be someone to please, trampling your own needs. All require continuous maintenance because none of these false selves fulfill our need for validation. God is the only one who can give you validation.

Our true selves begin to grow only when we realize our brokenness, confronting the false selves we hide behind, surrendering all to Jesus. John Eldredge writes in *Restoration Year*, "Your false self is never wholly false. Those gifts you've been using are often quite true about you, but you've used them to hide behind. The power is in your true self. When you begin to offer not merely your gifts but your true self— this is when you become powerful. That is the place God can come in and heal, and the glory of your creation will shine."[2]

In California, there is a rush to cover up any signs of aging even before the beauty of youth begins to fade—Botox treatments conceal the first sign of wrinkles, a lid lift for the eyes, a tummy tuck and breast enhancement to improve the figure. All these procedures become burdens to maintain as the aging process continues. Over time, instead of looking like real faces with expressions, faces are as frozen as a mannequin's.

Among other signs of aging, I have wrinkles—they tell the truth about me. I am old. I don't use Botox or surgery to disguise my wrinkles (though I do buy anti-wrinkle cream, despite knowing it doesn't work). Most of the time I like that my face is marked by experiences. I proudly wear these wrinkles, as they are the result of decades of smiling at children, parents, and teachers.

As John Eldredge wrote, "In this forest of fig leaves, where you are never sure you are getting the true person, there is nothing false about Jesus."[3]

As King David wrote toward the end of his life, "I know, my God, that you test the heart and have pleasure in uprightness. In the uprightness of my heart I have freely offered all these things, and now I have seen your people, who are present here, offering freely and joyously to you" (I Chronicles 29:17).

FORGIVENESS

Forgiveness is not about the other person, forgiveness is all about you, tied to the blessings that follow. I know this from personal experience. As I chose to forgive GK, in obedience to biblical wisdom, family relationships were healed. In contrast, repressed anger manifests in your body as pain or sickness or harmful actions. Without forgiveness, over time all you have is an assortment of broken relationships. Forgiveness is about your journey—God building you up to be a better person, the one he created you to be, to live a life of joy and peace. "Forgive us our sins, for we ourselves forgive everyone who is indebted to us" (Luke 11:4).

SPIRITUAL HARMONY WITH GOD

Your eighties can be the best of times. Everywhere I go, women of all ages exclaim they want to be like me when they grow old. Why? Living from the wisdom within reflects God's glory drawing everyone to him! "Even youths grow tired and weary, and young men stumble and fall; but those who hope in the LORD will renew their strength. They will soar on wings like eagles; they will run and not grow weary, and they will walk and not be faint" (Isaiah 40:30–31).

I spend each morning on my patio, overlooking the Saddleback Mountains, spending time alone with God, thanking and praising him, praying, and meditating on Scripture, listening like one being instructed. Over time, by hanging out with Jesus soaking up his Word, a wonderful sense of inner peace and joy invades the soul.

Death to self and life with Jesus is the only path to inner peace and joy. "You keep him in perfect peace whose mind is stayed on you, because he trusts in you" (Isaiah 26:3). Inner peace and oneness with Jesus help us see others as Jesus does, robed in his righteousness, increasing our love, and restoring harmony.

In *The Way of a Warrior*, Erwin McManus wrote "where there is inner peace, all relations are made right and everything is made whole. When we are broken, all we have left is the pieces of our true selves. This results in selfish self taking control with a flood of unhealthy behaviors such as anger, rage, greed, deception, and an assortment of addictive behaviors."[4]

KNOWING HIS PRESENCE

With inner peace comes wisdom. As Solomon instructs us, "My son, if you receive my words and treasure up my commandments with you, making your ear attentive to wisdom and inclining your heart to understanding ... Then you will understand righteousness and justice and equity, every good path; for wisdom will come into your heart, and knowledge will be pleasant to your soul" (Proverbs 2:1–2, 9–10).

How do you become a woman who is wise within? Becoming wise is a long, painful process that comes to fruition as you finally come to the end of yourself by surrendering all to Jesus Christ, your Lord and Savior. Out of reverence and respect, you cooperate with Jesus by being deliberate and disciplined, spending time every day in relationship with him. This requires solitude, silence, prayer, and saturating your mind with Scripture, asking him to illuminate it for you. These conditions are essential for hearing the gentle whisper of God.

The wise woman aims to live each day in the presence of God—to feel his love, seek to please him, and reflect his glory. Since the Garden of Eden, man's main problem has been sin. As children of God, though, we have been freed from the burden of sin, for there is no condemnation of those who are in Christ (Romans:8:1). As Paul wrote, "So we do not lose heart. Though our outer self is wasting away, our inner self is being renewed day by day" (2 Corinthians 4:16). What a marvelous truth. The body is declining, and the mind may be slipping as well, but the spirit is transformed with love and inner strength. Your living relationship with Jesus helps you approach each day with confidence, his direction and guidance.

> And I will lead the blind in a way that they do not know, in paths that they have not known I will guide them. I will turn the darkness before them into light, the rough places into level ground. These are the things I do, and I do not forsake them. (Isaiah 42:16)

Breaking free from faulty self-images you hide behind, you will see yourself as God sees you—radiant in the righteousness, and wrapped in the luminous love, of Jesus. Your identity as "Bless the LORD, O my soul, and forget not all his benefits, who forgives all your iniquity, who heals all your diseases, who redeems your life from the pit, who crowns you with steadfast love and mercy, who satisfies you with good so that your youth is renewed like the eagles" (Psalm 103:2–5).

THE CIRCLE OF LOVE

As Jesus lives in us, we become increasingly confident in his love for us. Since our love is sourced from God's love, his love reaches full expression when we love others. Not just some, but all others. "We love because he first loved us. If anyone says, "I love God," and hates his brother, he is a liar; for he who does not love his brother whom he has seen cannot love God whom he has not seen. And this commandment we have from him: whoever loves God must also love his brother" (1 John 4:19–21). As you walk with Jesus you look back and realize that is exactly what he has accomplished in your life.

The deepest wounds are often inflicted in family relationships. When the Holy Spirit first convinced me to forgive my husband, who was a serial adulterer, I felt this request of me to give so freely after being inflicted with such suffering was harsh and unkind. Only later did I realize the truth and wisdom of these words. Ever since, I have been reaping the harvest. I feel Jesus was with me in the pain and blessed me abundantly. The wise woman has a clean slate. She has forgiven herself and others, enjoys loving relationships, and lives in the peace and joy of the spirit.

The Bible is God's love letter, taught to us by those whose lives have the fragrance of Jesus. I am glad the Good Lord blessed me with a long life so my family and friends can witness a version of me closer to what God intended. Being at one with Jesus by the power of the Holy Spirit, his light shines through us to bless the lives of others. They'll ask how you did it and you'll declare, "The Lord did it all. As I decreased, he increased. If he can do it for me, he can do it for you. Blessed be the name of the Lord."

CHRIST CRUCIFIED

Oswald Chambers's words regarding the cross sum up its beauty and profundity. He says, "The greatest note of triumph ever sounded in the ears of a startled universe was the sound on the Cross of Christ—'It is finished!'" (John 19:30). "That is the final word in the redemption of humankind."[5] Such redemption influences all relationships, however, because of the work of the cross, one's relationship to Christ becomes the most integral of all life's relationships. Chambers says, "There is only one relationship that really matters, and that is your personal relationship to your personal Redeemer and Lord. If you maintain that at all costs, letting everything else go, God will fulfill His purpose through your life."[6]

I have found this to be true in my life and you will too. Everything falls into place when Jesus is the most important relationship in your life. Your relationships are kind and caring, your purpose is enhanced as you grow and are guided by Jesus. Seek biblical wisdom, stay close to Jesus by choosing to obey his Word, and he will transform your life. Live victoriously, living every minute with Jesus.

> For I delivered to you as of first importance what I also received: that Christ died for our sins in accordance with the Scriptures, that he was buried, that he was raised on the third day in accordance with the Scriptures. (1 Corinthians 15:3–4)

As John Eldredge writes in *Restoration Year*, "God wants to live this life together with you, to share in your days and decisions, your desires and disappointments. He wants intimacy with you in the midst of the madness and mundane, the meetings and memos, the laundry and lists, the projects and pain. He wants to pour his love into your heart, that center place within that is the truest you. He is not interested in intimacy with the person you think you are supposed to be. He wants intimacy with the real you—who you are now."[7] You are the Wise Woman Within.

PRACTICES TO PONDER

1. Am I loving my family, friends, and neighbors as I want to be loved?

2. Am I living my daily life with Jesus allowing his love and light to flow through me to others?

3. Am I freely sharing the Good News of the gospel?

PRAYER

And so, from the day we heard, we have not ceased to pray for you, asking that you may be filled with the knowledge of his will in all spiritual wisdom and understanding, so as to walk in a manner worthy of the Lord, fully pleasing to him: bearing fruit in every good work and increasing in the knowledge of God; being strengthened with all power, according to his glorious might, for all endurance and patience with joy; giving thanks to the Father, who has qualified you to share in the inheritance of the saints in light. He has delivered us from the domain of darkness and transferred us to the kingdom of his beloved Son, in whom we have redemption, the forgiveness of sins. (Colossians 1:9–14)

—CHAPTER TWENTY-ONE—
THE WISE WOMAN WITHIN

Those who are wise shall shine like the brightness of the
sky above; and those who turn many to righteousness,
like the stars forever and ever. (Daniel 12:3)

GROWING UP—LIVING AND SPEAKING THE TRUTH

As we grasp who we are in Christ, we find the Wise
Woman Within is the very soul of who we are—the invisible
but very real part of us that God mixed with dust and Spirit
to create our unique selves. She is the part of us in tune
with the Holy Spirit and when we listen to her, we feel
peace, we feel loved—balanced and excited to be alive.
Behind her eyes, we see things from a higher perspective,
understanding the bigger picture, showing us what to do
and what to say. Worry drops away, calm descends. We see
ourselves, others, and circumstances more clearly, as the
fog lifts in the sunlight of authentic truth telling.

The prophet Isaiah alluded to this voice in the Old
Testament. "And your ears shall hear a word behind you,
saying, 'This is the way, walk in it,' when you turn to the
right or when you turn to the left" (Isaiah 30:21).

The Wise Woman Within (WWW), in essence, is the
combination of the Holy Spirit connecting with your unique
personality, your feminine soul. It manifests when we quiet

ourselves and open our hearts to listen—no easy trick in this noisy and list-oriented world.

We sometimes think of our relationship to God as little humans looking up and straining to hear a God who lives way up high. But the miracle of Christ's message is "Christ in us, the hope of glory." Where does God live? Within. He is as close as our breath, but we must tap into him, as a branch to the vine. When we do, the WWW speaks, each day aligning with what the Spirit breathes into us.

We desire that our spirit, body, and words are aligned with that attunement of the Word, the Spirit, and the Word made flesh (Jesus). We find ourselves drawn toward understanding ourselves in the likeness of the trinity, the various aspects of ourselves desiring to work together in unison. We find our words want to match the Word, our thoughts his thoughts, our ways his ways, and we begin to recognize our desire to be his child and our great inability to achieve his divine perfection. There, we stop grasping and start receiving grace. Our efforts become that of love, when the end of ourselves meets God himself and we extend that understanding outward. Then we can offer forgiveness and grace as we've received. We know the difference between forgiveness and saying "no" to accept something not of God. We understand where we end and others begin and know what is healthy for us and what is not.

We find our need and reverence for this mighty savior God who is anything but human, as we are human, and thus is worthy of our praise and life worship. We find ourselves more mature and unified with others in this effort—partners in the endeavor of growing together. We are no longer infantile, thinking as the world thinks, but we are grown heirs to the throne of truth, now apostles of that truth. This is the calling of Ephesians when it says,

And he gave the apostles, the prophets, the evangelists, the shepherds and teachers, to equip the saints for the work of ministry, for building up the body of Christ, until we all attain to the unity of the faith and of the knowledge of the Son of God, to mature manhood, to the measure of the stature of the fullness of Christ, so that we may no longer be children, tossed to and fro by the waves and carried about by every wind of doctrine, by human cunning, by craftiness in deceitful schemes. Rather, speaking the truth in love, we are to grow up in every way into him who is the head, into Christ, from whom the whole body, joined and held together by every joint with which it is equipped, when each part is working properly, makes the body grow so that it builds itself up in love. (Ephesians 4:11–16)

Oneness with God is our goal and our destiny. In some of his last words to his disciples and us, Jesus prayed,

I do not ask for these only, but also for those who will believe in me through their word, that they may all be one, just as you, Father, are in me, and I in you, that they also may be in us, so that the world may believe that you have sent me. The glory that you have given me I have given to them, that they may be one even as we are one, I in them and you in me, that they may become perfectly one, so that the world may know that you sent me and loved them even as you loved me. (John 17:20–23)

ALL ACTIONS CONCERN ME

The church is catholic, universal, so are all her actions; all that she does belongs to all. When she baptizes a child, that action concerns me; for that child is thereby connected to that body which is my head too and engrafted into that body whereof I am a member. And when she buries a man, that action concerns me: all mankind is of one author, and is one volume; when one man dies, one chapter is not torn out of the book, but translated into a better language; and every chapter

> must be so translated; God employs several translators; some pieces are translated by age, some by sickness, some by war, some by justice; but God's hand is in every translation, and his hand shall bind up all our scattered leaves again for that library where every book shall lie open to one another.—John Donne, "Meditation 17"[1]

Sixteenth-century writer and church cleric John Donne beautifully states the timelessness of such wisdom—one day all the leaves that are each of our lives will be bound up as pages of God's book, where we will once for all lie open before him and to one another—restoration as was intended in the beginning, a beautiful reconciliation of the original plan.

After losing his wife and recognizing his own imminent death, John Donne wrote this beautiful piece discussing the role of an individual's life in light of the universal and the eternal. He recognizes the importance of the individual's decision and how each decision has a ripple effect on the rest of humanity at large, both in one's own temporal life, and in those years and time outside of his temporal existence. Donne's work is still widely cited four centuries later by prominent authors and figures (Milton and Hemingway, among others) and, as a believer, Donne's work and influence is established on earth and now translated as a saint in the glory of heaven.

I (Jess) love that Donne discusses death as "translation." We often don't discuss the purpose of death in society, but doesn't death have the ability to say so much about the person who has passed and about those left to mourn and celebrate? Doesn't death do so much? Doesn't death always usher in something new? Death also shows us both our desperate frailty and our unbelievable significance—one man's death makes life drastically smaller, while another's birth makes life significantly bigger. This is why I believe

Donne goes on in his work in "Meditation 17" to say the death bells toll for those who have ears to hear, and why God asks us to remember that our days are numbered—and to keep that in mind as we live to gain wisdom.

Recently my husband, Andy, our two kids, and I traveled to East Tennessee to spend time with our extended family over Christmas break. Our little family of four set out on a short hike around an old rock quarry which had, when it was drilled decades ago, erupted with water that now forms a beautiful, tranquil lake. On that chilly morning, fallen leaves were layered and wet underfoot, melted snow making little mud puddles on the trail. It was so beautiful to see leaves in their process of death and transformation. Once high overhead and vibrantly green, these leaves, which had fallen and became stiff, brown, and dry, were compacted over months and now returning to the earth.

The process was breathtaking as we could see this tender moment of transformation where the leaf was both partially its old self—a leaf, and partially what it would be—nutrient-rich soil, a garden bed. From this mud would one day come another new pine, filling the earth with beauty, life, and air to breathe. I was reminded we need to embrace and appreciate, even esteem, those failures and deaths in our lives that sting, understanding that life comes out of non-life in God. We need to remember the digging down of the soul, if we can withstand the drilling, will erupt into life-giving water. This is his design. He is the God who is able to miraculously breathe life from non-life.

We also are in process like the leaves, and can trust that every season has purpose, worth, and dignity beyond our life, beyond our very limited understanding.

A new truth lives any time something is shed, or some old idea or addiction or fear dies, and in its place, we receive grace and the life-giving lesson it gives. We decide to put to rest that which is no longer working and begin to live anew. Almost always this requires death of some kind followed by a transcendent rebirth.

LIVING FROM WISDOM, FOR ALWAYS

> So teach us to number our days that we may get a heart of wisdom. (Psalm 90:12)

Living in authenticity and in pursuit of Godly wisdom is living with an understanding of one's place in the origin of all things, within the canon of time. Authentic living is a sacred understanding of one's life, with its beginning, middle, and temporary end, as an integral, cherished, and loved part. Living from an authentic place is both fully acting upon, and submitting to the author of, the biblical canon of life, appreciating the wonder of it all—we are part of this amazing story.

Living authentically is committing, moment by moment, to understanding the purpose for which God created you for the duration of your brief life on this earth. In pursuing this purpose and truth, one aims to be trustworthy and genuine. "Being" influences "doing." Heart follows body and body follows heart. You do what you are, and you are what you do. When we are hung-up in trials and failures, the truth to which we are tethered quickly draws us back, and we are anchored in peace equipped with many well-fought resources.

Authenticity is living in hope for now and beyond, that when the book of your life is closed, the sequel will open to the pages of heaven, where we will live in community with God, our heavenly father, and with our authentic family, forever after. We will fully embrace who we were meant to be.

The excitement of heaven is of fully reaching our authentic, true inner self, though until then, we will continue to grow in wisdom with practice, in listening, and with discernment. The day of arrival will be glorious because we will fully know and understand the divine connection into which we were born, welcomed, and established forever in God's family, as God intended from the beginning. Sin will be washed away and replaced with splendor and unity. To know we are worth this process—of freedom, refinement, and ultimate union and acceptance—is the story of God.

ABOUT THE AUTHORS

JEAN BARNES

A veteran educator, Jean is highly esteemed for her expertise in diagnosing behavior and learning problems, developing successful strategies to solve these difficulties, while helping parents and teachers to implement change. Barnes brings an impressive résumé as a leader in diagnostic individual learning, home and school collaboration, and character education in eight outstanding school districts across the country.

- Intermediate leader of ungraded individualized learning team
- Awarded a series of grants to implement "Raising Kids with Character" programs at the elementary level.

- Her model program, *Family Growth Seminars*, earned a grant by the state of Connecticut and was published in *Promising Practices in Special Education and Student Services*. This led to professional seminars for counselors and psychologists throughout the state.

- *Love and Discipline: Keys to Effective Discipline* selected to be presented at the National Association of School Psychologist in 1996.

- *The Parent Teacher Connection: Strengthening the Link* was presented at the National Association of School Psychologist in 1997.

Jean writes from experience as a mother and grandmother. As a mom in a variety of roles married, divorced, and raising her sons on her own, remarried, and parenting a blended family.

Jean earned a bachelors of science degree from the University of Wisconsin in Madison in child development, a masters of education from the University of Cincinnati in counseling and a certificate of advanced study in psychology from Fairfield University. Her doctoral studies in marriage and family therapy, as well as human development at the University of Connecticut, shaped her principles that helped children thrive.

Jean is the author of *Purposeful Parenting: Six Steps to Bring Out the Best in Your Kids* (Shippensburg, PA: Destiny Image Publishers, 2015). Based on biblical wisdom and best practices in psychology, *Purposeful Parenting* tells you how to love and discipline your child while guiding us to inject purpose and meaning into the life of each child.

JESSICA WRASMAN

Jessica grew up in the mountains of Southern California. She earned her BA and MA at Concordia University Irvine in California. In their early marriage, she and her husband lived and taught in Hangzhou, China. She taught English courses where they lived and worked on campus at Hangzhou DIanzi Keji Daxue (Hanzghou University of Technology). They would ride an electric bike forty-five minutes through the city, population ten million, to attend worship and teach Sunday school at Hangzhou International Christian fellowship, where people from all nations gathered to worship in English. While in Hangzhou, local newspapers and magazines published Jessica's articles on local spots of interest and various events in the city for ex-pats living in Hangzhou.

Returning stateside, Jessica taught World Literature and English Literature at Crean Lutheran high School in Irvine, California. She then returned to Concordia University Irvine where she taught English courses.

During those life transitions and moments, Jessica became increasingly aware of the need for inner healing work, realizing that her personal healing of past emotional traumas would be paramount to her ability to be of love and service to others. Since having children, she has focused primarily on life at home, while also doing some freelance editing and the writing of *Wise Woman Within*. She also serves in ministry. In her travels, opportunities, and traumas, Jessica learned the truth of God's words of Romans 8:28, "We know that in all things God works for the good of those who love Him, who have been called according to His purpose" (NIV).

ENDNOTES

Preface

1. Nancy Tillman, *On the Night You Were Born* (New York, NY: Feiwel and Friends, 2005), 23, 27.

Chapter 1

1. A. L. Rowse, *The Annotated Shakespeare.* William Shakespeare. *Hamlet* (New York, NY: Octavian Books Limited, 1978), 205.

2. Brené Brown, *The Gifts of Imperfection: Letting Go of Who We Think We Should Be and Embracing Who We Are* (Center City, MN: Hazelden, 2010), 26.

Chapter 2

1. John Eldredge, *Beautiful Outlaw* (New York, Boston, Nashville: Faithwords, 2013), 146.

2. Peter Scarrero, *Emotionally Healthy Spirituality* (Grand Rapids, MI: Zondervan, 2014), 145.

3. Oswald Chambers, *My Utmost to His Highest* (Grand Rapids, MI: Discovery House Publishers, 1992), January, 23.

Chapter 4

1. John Trent, *Life Mapping: A Helpful Hands-On Process for Overcoming Your Past* (Colorado Springs, CO: Waterbrook Press, 1998).

2. Leo Tolstoy, Margaret Lock, Aylmer Maude, and Louise Maude. 1986. *How much land does a man need?* (Brisbane, QLD: Locks' Press, 1986).

3. Ruth Chou Simmons, *Gracelaced* (Eugene, OR: Harvest House Publishers, 2017), 15.

4. John Eldredge, *Restoration Year: A 365 Day Devotional* (Nashville, TN: Thomas Nelson Publishing, 2018), 284.

Chapter 5

1. Allen, Woody, director (1977). *Annie Hall* (United Artists).

2. Murray Bowen, *Family Therapy in Clinical Practice* (New York, NY: Jason Aronson, Inc., 1978), 472–73.

Chapter 7

1. Jean Barnes, *Purposeful Parenting: Six Steps to Bring Out the Best in Your Kids* (Shippensburg, PA: Destiny Image Publishers, 2015).

2. Brené Brown, *Rising Strong* (New York: Spiegel & Grau, 2015), 40–41.

Chapter 8

1. Fincher, David (2008). *The Curious Case of Benjamin Button* (Paramount Pictures).

2. Allender, Dan, Tremper Longman III, *Bold Love*, (Colorado Springs, CO: Nav Press, Publishing Ministry of Navigators, 1992), 142.

3. Leeana Tankersley, *Begin Again* (Grand Rapids, MI: Revel, 2018), 16.

Note: I (Jess) was first introduced to St. Benedict's quote in the book *Begin Again* where Tankersley discusses this Benedictine mantra as a way of centering oneself in grace and love to move forward from a place of gentle acceptance and peace. I am citing her book here as this is the place where I found it, while there are numerous other resources which have used this sixth century monk's timeless words.

Chapter 9

1. John Calvin, *Institutes of the Christian Religion*, trans. Henry Beveridge (Grand Rapids, MI: Eerdmans, 1959), 37.

2. Jerry Briggs, *The Practice of Godliness* (Colorado Springs, CO Nav Press, Publishing Ministry of Navigators, 2008).

3. Oswald Chambers, *My Utmost for His Highest* (New York, NY: Dodd, Mead and Co., 1963), 219.

4. Tayari Jones, "Sunday Review: What Mandela Lost," *The New York Times* (New York, NY), July 8, 2018.

Chapter 10

1. Paul Tillich, "What Suffering Does." NYTimes.com, April 7, 2014. Accessed 2-25-2021.

Chapter 11

1. Loren Toussaint, Grant S. Shields, Gabriel Dorn, George M. Slavich. "Effects of lifetime stress exposure on mental and physical health in young adulthood: How stress degrades and forgiveness protects health." *Journal of health psychology* 21, no. 6 (June 2016): 1004-1014 https://scholar.google.com/citations?view_op=view_citation&hl=en&user=TM4jXwwAAAAJ&citation_for_view=TM4jXwwAAAAJ:_Qo2XoVZTnwC

Chapter 12

1. Jane Austen, *Pride and Prejudice* (New York, NY: Modern Library, 1995), 301.

Chapter 13

1. Erik Erikson, *Identity: Youth in Crisis.* New York: Norton & Company, Inc, 1968), 133–35.

2. John M. Gottman, *The Seven Principles for Making Marriage Work*, (New York, NY: Harmony Books, 2015), 32–37.

3. Robert Weiss, *Staying the Course*, (New York, NY: Free Press, 1990)

4. Allender, Longman III, *Bold Love*, 88.

5. Allender, Longman III, 162.

Chapter 14

1. Ruth Chou Simmons, *Gracelaced*, 151.

2. Martin Luther King, Jr. "Advice for Living: Nov. 1957" in *The Papers of Martin Luther King, Jr. Volume IV: Symbol of the Movement, January 1957–December 1958*, eds. Clayborn Carson, Susan Carson, Adrienne Clay, Virginia Shadron, and Kieran Taylor, (Berkeley, CA: University of California Press at Berkeley and Los Angles, 2000), 306.

3. Kristen Weir, "Forgiveness Can Improve Mental and Physical Health," *CE Corner*, Vol. 48, No. 1, American Psychological Association, www.apa.org, 30. Accessed 2-28-21.

4. Rick Warren, The Decade of Destiny, live sermon. (Lake Forest, CA), September 2011.

5. Barnes, *Purposeful Parenting: Six Steps to Bring Out the Best in Your Kids.*

Chapter 15

1. John Burke, *Image Heaven: Near-Death Experiences, God's Promises, and the Exhilarating Future that Awaits You,* (Ada, MI: Baker Books, 2015).

2. Chambers, *My Utmost for His Highest* 1963, November29.

3. John M. Gottman, *The Seven Principles for Making Marriage Work,* 4–5.

4. John M. Gottman, *The Seven Principles for Making Marriage Work,* 19.

Chapter 16

1. Brené Brown, *Braving the Wilderness: The Quest for True Belonging and the Courage to Stand Alone* (New York: Random House, 2017), 38–39.

2. P. A. Cowan, C. P. Cowan, M. Kline Pruett. & K. Pruett. (2019) Fathers' and Mothers' Attachment Styles, Couple Conflict, Parenting Quality, and Children's Behavior Problems: an Intervention Test of Meditation. *Attachment*

and Human Development. <https://doi.org/10.1080/146167 34.2019.1582600.>

Chapter 17

1. Mary Oliver, "Wild Geese." *New and Selected Poems* (Boston, Massachusetts: Beacon Press, 1992), 110.

2. Chambers, *My Utmost for His Highest*, 1963, August 6th.

3. Scazzero. *Emotionally Healthy Spirituality* 148.

4. L.B. Cowman, *Streams in the Desert* (Grand Rapids, MI: Zondervan, 1997), 256.

5. Eldredge, *Restoration Year: A 365 Day Devotional*, 20.

6. Chambers, *My Utmost for His Highest* 1963, December 7

7 Andrew Murray, *Abide in Christ* (New Kensington, PA: Whitaker House, 2002), 62.

Chapter 18

1. Mary Oliver, "The Fourth Sign of the Zodiac," *Blue Horses* (New York, NY: Penguin, 2014), 61.

2. *Webster's New Twentieth Century Dictionary*, (Collins World; 2nd edition, 1975), s.v. "Authentic."

3. Sue Monk Kidd, *When the Heart Waits*, (New York, NY: Harper One, 2006), 182.

4. Charles Dollen, *The Book of Catholic Wisdom* (Our Sunday Visitor Pub. Division), 152.

5. Charles Stanley, *In Touch: Daily Readings for Devoted Living* monthly mailing pamphlet devotional (Atlanta, GA: April, 2020), 36.

6. Chambers, *My Utmost for His Highest* 1963, September 20.

7. Sue Monk Kidd, *When the Heart Waits*, 200.

8. Aeschylus Quotes. BrainyQuote.com, BrainyMedia Inc, 2021. <https://www.brainyquote.com/quotes/ aeschylus_148591>, accessed February 25, 2021.

9. Tracy Ellis Ross, "Michelle Obama and Tracee Ellis Ross on the Power of Women's Stories," interview by Philip Galanes, *New York Times*, November 20, 2018.

10. Harold Bloom, Harper Lee, *Harper Lee's To Kill a Mockingbird* (E-book, Facts on File, Inc., 2010), 81.

11. Natalie Angliger, "Scientists Mull Role of Empathy in Man and Beast." *New York Times,* May 9, 1995.

12. Diana Baumrind, "High Demands, Great Support: Authoritative Parenting in a Nutshell," in *Parenting for Character Five Experts, Five Practices*, ed. David Streight, (Portland, OR: Council for Spiritual and Ethical Education, 2008), 17–21.

Chapter 19

1. Sue Monk Kidd, *Firstlight* (New York, NY: Penguin, 2007), 37.

Chapter 20

1. Mary Oliver, "The Summer Day" *New and Selected Poems* (Boston, MA: Beacon Press, 1992), <loc.gov>, 2-25-2021.

2. Eldredge, *Restoration Year: A 365 Day Devotional*, 58.

3. Eldredge, *Restoration Year: A 365 Day Devotional*, 225.

4. Erwin McManus, *The Way of the Warrior* (New York: Waterbrook, 2019), 8.

5. Chambers, *My Utmost for His Highest* 1963, November 21.

6. Chambers, *My Utmost for His Highest* 1963, November 30.

7. Eldredge, *Restoration Year: A 365 Day Devotional*, 18.

Chapter 21

1. John Donne, "Meditation 17," in *The Works of John Donne. vol III*, ed. Henry Alford, (London: John W. Parker, 1839), 574–75.

Made in the USA
Columbia, SC
13 June 2022